ETHICAL MANAGING

Rules and Results

F. Neil Brady

San Diego State University

ETHICAL MANAGING

Rules and Results

MACMILLAN PUBLISHING COMPANY
NEW YORK
Collier Macmillan Publishers
LONDON

Macmillan Publishing Company
866 Third Avenue, New York, New York 10022

Collier Macmillan Canada, Inc.

LIBRARY OF CONGRESS CATALOGING-IN-PUBLICATION DATA

Brady, F. Neil
    Ethical managing : rules and results / F. Neil Brady.
        p.   cm.
    Bibliography: p.
    Includes index.
    ISBN 0-02-313341-4
    1. Business ethics.   2. Management—Moral and ethical aspects.
    I.   Title.
    HF5387.B69   1990
    174′4—dc20   89-31477
                                                                           CIP

Printing: 3 4 5 6 7 8   Year: 3 4 5 6 7 8

Book Team

Acquisition Editor: Charles Stewart
Production Supervisor: Jennifer Carey
Production Manager: Nick Sklitsis
Text Designer: Patrice Fodero
Cover Designer: Brian Sheridan
Cover photograph: Giraudon/Art Resources
Illustrations: Laura Maestro Hartman

This book was set in ITC New Baskerville by V & M Graphics and was printed and bound by Hamilton Printing Company. The cover was printed by Phoenix Color Corp.

Preface

With all of the newspaper and television accounts of scandals
in government and business, there is plenty of evidence that
from the practical perspective the teaching of ethics in schools
of management is in need of either repair or revitalization.
This assumes, of course, that the teaching of ethics has something to offer to meet this need, and the questioning of this
assumption is a motivational starting point for this book. Having taught management ethics for several years, I have been
repeatedly frustrated by the practical mismatch between management problems and moral philosophy. I'm not certain that
the abbreviated and unexamined versions of ethical theory, as
typically presented in business ethics texts, are getting us
where we want to go. I am convinced that good managers
employ ethical theoretic thinking almost routinely and that organizational policies and procedures are permeated by it. This
book is an attempt to demonstrate the truth of this claim. Unless we can connect ethical theory more closely with management practice, we may be dressing our business curriculum
windows with philosophical finery but failing to meet the urgent need for clarity of thought in management ethics.

This need for the development and elaboration of ethical
theory was documented in a February 1988 report by the
Ethics Resource Center (Washington, D.C.) titled "Ethics Education in American Business Schools," which reported the re-

sults of a survey of undergraduate and graduate school deans. It observed that "ethical theory is the topic mentioned most frequently by respondents as needing new or continued research" (p. 2).

This book begins with the assumption that improved research and teaching in management ethics is badly needed. But it begins also with the methodological assumption that good thinking in management ethics is already being done by many practitioners and scholars; all that remains to be done is simply to describe what they do. Therefore, the forms of the development of ethical theory taken in this book owe more to my need to describe what good thinkers in business do than to a need to elaborate an abstract and consistent theory. The book can perhaps be described as a collection of observations that have led to a more practical development of ethical theory.

People with more focused interests may not find this book wholly satisfying. Philosophers, who typically require rigorous logical development of ideas, may complain about the lack of detailed argumentation. Management practitioners, who need quick help with present problems, may find the existing argumentation burdensome and confusing. And management students who are looking for clear solutions in ethics will remain frustrated over the lack of closure for ethical dilemmas. But what all of them (especially students) should remember is that what we search for in ethics is an understanding of perfection in human maturity; out of respect for ourselves, that knowledge shouldn't be too easy to acquire.

Pedagogically speaking, I have used all of this material at the graduate and undergraduate levels, and the students — especially undergraduates — find it challenging, in particular, Chapters Five, Six, and Seven. I have resisted the urge to try to oversimplify this material too much on the grounds that what managers do when they make ethical decisions is itself very difficult; excessive simplification would therefore misrepresent the decision-making reality of the managerial world. However, there are at least three things that make the book more accessible to students. First, the questions, cases, and exercises at the end of each chapter are not just thrown in at the request of the publisher; they have been collected over the years as they relate to the material discussed in the chapters. The exercises are almost as important for the overall argument of the book as the chapters themselves. Rather than use the chapters to demonstrate endlessly the practical relevance of the ideas presented, I rely on the exercises to provide a demonstration of the applied nature of the concepts in each chapter. So, don't ignore the exercises; they are an integral part of the book.

Second, a Summary of Key Concepts is provided at the end of each chapter. These summaries help to condense and simplify the material so that the reader can see at a glance what each chapter contains.

Third, an Instructor's Manual is available for those using this book as a text in a course. This manual not only provides plenty of advice and instruction for helping the students read the book, it also supplies examination material (multiple-choice and essay questions). I also urge instructors not to ignore the diagnostic test provided in the Appendix to the book. It is the single best thing I do with my students each semester, and it quickly engages students in discussions of ethical theory.

Much of the material in this book has grown out of research conducted and published over the last 5 or 6 years. I thank the *Academy of Management Review* and the *Journal of Business Ethics* for permission to incorporate in this book revisions of earlier published material:

a. "A Janus-Headed Model of Ethical Theory: Looking Two Ways at Business/Society Issues," *The Academy of Management Review*, V. 10 (1985), pp. 568–576.

b. "Practical Formalism: A New Methodological Proposal in Business Ethics," *Journal of Business Ethics*, V. 7 (1988), pp. 163–170.

c. "Rules for Making Exceptions to Rules," *The Academy of Management Review*, V. 12 (1987), pp. 436–444. (This essay won the "Best Paper of 1987" Award from *The Academy of Management Review*.)

d. "The Aesthetic Components of Management Ethics," *The Academy of Management Review*, V. 11 (1986), pp. 337–344.

I also thank my students, Sara Copeland and Janine Richey, for their helpful reviews of the manuscript. And I appreciate the timely encouragement and advice from Kirk Hart and Peter Mills.

F.N.B.

Table of Contents

C H A P T E R

1

A Brief Introduction

It is common to suppose that managerial decisions are seldom ethical—that is, they seldom raise the question of ethics. We expect them often to be legal questions. In such situations, the manager consults with a corporate attorney. Managerial decisions are also often political judgments. Here one seeks the advice of trusted counselors, friends, or political advisors. And when managerial decisions relate to matters of efficiency and effectiveness, one seeks the help of technical staff with the appropriate training and abilities. Similarly, one might suppose that from time to time a manager's decision is related to an ethical issue, and one would look to trusted associates for advice.

If this view is correct, ethics would be a minor concern for the modern manager. Ethical issues would arise no more often than, say, legal issues, and when they do, help could be sought from an appropriate specialist. Therefore, ethics would become a secondary concern for managers, and one that is far less important than the often weightier concerns of politics and law.

But this view assumes that managerial decisions represent discrete types: that some decisions refer to legal issues, others to merely political issues, and so on. And I suppose it is not altogether wrong to think of managerial decisions in this way. Surely, for any given issue, some forms of advice will be more relevant than others. For example, if a manager were negotiating a union contract, a judgment regarding the comparative strength of one's position is crucial; the law, ethics, and financial position might all be additional considerations, but in a negotiating session politics is paramount. So, one would not be wholly misguided to suppose that ethical matters make only occasional demands on the modern manager.

But what this leaves open is the possibility that although any given decision may reflect the dominating influence of, say, political or legal matters, every managerial decision may exhibit some significant ethical component, and some decisions may be dominated by ethical concerns. Indeed, one of the purposes of this chapter is to promote increased awareness of the extensive claim that ethics has upon even the routine daily decisions of the modern manager. The job of managing is permeated by ethics, from the level of the smallest personal decisions to the largest public policies. And depending on how one feels about the priority of ethical claims on one's behavior, ethics may be a first and necessary criterion for decision making, even when ethical requirements are easy to meet and the decision turns on some other more elusive need.

Arguments for the Centrality of Ethics

Instead of thinking of ethics as only a tangential concern for modern managers, it may be more realistic to regard most managerial decisions as permeated by ethics. Managers are powerful, and where there is power, there is potential for good and evil. In what follows, several reasons are listed for supposing managerial decision making to be fundamentally concerned with ethics.

Managerial decisions affect persons' lives and well-being. Think of the following kinds of issues that face managers daily:

1. Which one of five eligible persons should get the promotion?

2. How can I diffuse the discontent on the shop floor among angry and frustrated workers?

3. What position should I take in negotiating with the union?

4. Should I try to arrange a private office for a particularly successful employee?

5. Should I assign two people whose personalities differ to the same project team?

For all of the preceding issues, a wrong decision results in conditions that are considerably less favorable than they could have been. When managers make a wrong decision and should have known better, we say that they were negligent, biased, or at least unwise. If they made the incorrect decision to promote their own interests, we often say that they were unethical.

We often describe situations, however, as being ethical even when we would not necessarily expect a manager to know how to respond. We may not even know the right answer ourselves; nevertheless, the situation may be an ethical one. Consider, for example, the need to decide whether to place two persons on the same project team. Such a matter is always an ethical issue, whether or not we would also describe the manager making that decision as ethical. It implies success or failure of the team; it affects people's lives.

Indeed, any issue that implies significant harm or benefit to others may be described as ethical. On grounds that will become more familiar later in this book, any situation that is less favorable than it could have been falls short ethically.

Managers must distribute organizational resources fairly.
It is a little easier to see why a manager's need to distribute resources is generated by ethical requirements. Consider the following situations:

1. How should I use our profits this year—to increase employee benefits, to lower the prices of our products, or to invest in new equipment?

2. Which of my employees should get the new chairs sent to us from the purchasing department?

3. How much time should I give to interviews with out-side groups, such as consumer groups, reporters, and community leaders?

4. How much money should the organization donate this year to community and political causes?

Such decisions are ethical because of the need to be fair, and fairness is a strong component of the daily managerial routine. But this is not as simple as it sounds. A fair distribution is not always an equal one. Special considerations often require that greater time or attention be given to one alternative. An employee with a back problem who did not get one of the new chairs allocated to the department might have legitimate reason to complain about being treated unfairly. Where special needs exist, there may be ethical justification for skewing an otherwise equal distribution in favor of those needs.

Managers design and implement rules and policies.
Another reason for thinking that a manager's daily routine is permeated by ethical issues is the manager's responsibility for organizational rules. The relationship of a manager to the rules is not merely mechanical. If it were, there would be no discretionary power, and there would be less reason for sup-posing the situation to be ethical. But because most managers do have discretion to wave rules or to change them, or at least to decide in any particular case whether a rule applies, we hold managers responsible for the proper development and application of organizational rules.

Consider the following typical managerial situations:

1. Should we adopt a policy regarding tardiness?

2. Should our policy regarding dress and grooming be used to urge Cynthia to avoid wearing provocative clothing?

3. Should the dress and grooming policy apply only to personnel who have contact with the public, or should it apply to all employees?

4. Are employees abusing their sick leave, and what should I do about it?

5. Is the policy regarding restricting the personal use of corporate automobiles effective, and what can be done when I suspect that someone is abusing that policy?

Managers both design and enforce organizational rules. The ethical responsibility in all of these situations is to produce a system of shared values and expectations that is realistic and fair.

Managerial decisions often test one's personal values. Finally, managerial decisions are often ethical because they put the manager's personal values to the test. The following examples illustrate such situations:

1. Should this report reflect my professional judgment or the requests of my boss?

2. Should I simply do what I'm told, even though I feel strongly otherwise?

3. Should I object to the sexual harassment in the office?

4. Should I be friends with others, if only for instrumental reasons?

5. My best friend is not well liked by our supervisor. Should I come to his defense in a matter, even though it might be seen as a personal challenge to our supervisor? Should I get involved in this problem?

6. Should I sacrifice time with my family to get ahead in my career?

Countless authors have drawn attention to the conflict between organizational and personal values and goals. Most persons who have spent any time in an organization have felt the tension.

This conflict between personal and organizational values may be as true for the modern mid-level manager as for anyone else. It is in the managerial arena that organizational dominance over personal judgment may be most intense. Managers are the link between organizational success and the lives of the individuals they supervise. Questions of organizational and personal conflict, therefore, tend to fall on the manager's shoulders.

So, there are several reasons why routine decisions of managers are permeated with questions of ethics.

Organization of This Book

Management ethics is a large topic, as we have seen. It covers issues ranging from small, one-on-one relationships to large public policy issues; from concrete cases to abstract principles. Almost anything a manager does holds ethical interest because the manager is always asking the question "What *should* I do?"

Given, then, that there is a lot to talk about when discussing management ethics, the next logical question becomes "How should that discussion proceed?" There are a variety of ways to "cut the pie." In most management ethics or business ethics books, the material is organized *topically*, following easily recognized major divisions. For example, common topical divisions include advertising ethics, environmental ethics, discrimination in the workplace, the relation of the individual to the organization, and so on. This vast array of topics or issues can be arranged in a variety of ways, as the growing number of business ethics textbooks make clear, but the overriding principle of division remains the same—topics.

Despite the abundant common sense of writing management ethics books from a topical perspective, there are some significant drawbacks. First, the issues in business ethics are not only numerous; they are also important and deserving of considerable thought. The best that can be hoped for in preparing a single work on management ethics topics is a shallow survey. There is the further risk that such a book will degenerate into a faddish collection of "in-the-news" issues that, although timely and interesting, may fail to address more abiding concerns.

Second, and more important, a topical orientation to management ethics is not necessarily a theoretical orientation. A survey of the issues, then, may not provide the kind of insight into the issues that may be made possible by some other orientation. What we all hunger for in business ethics is the satisfactory resolution of, or at least progress in resolving, difficult issues. A topical approach, however, undermines the contribution of theory by allowing intuitive, rather than theoretical, associations to guide the examination of issues. And this contributes to a common shortcoming of most discussions of business ethics, namely, the failure to supply insight beyond common intuition.

This book is different; it is *methodological*, rather than topical. It approaches the study of business ethics by focusing on the *techniques* people use to think about ethical issues, rather than on the issues themselves. Consequently, since the methods in business ethics are far fewer than the issues, this book can afford to take a close and detailed look at those methods without spreading itself too thin.

There are some drawbacks, however, to writing a book about methods in business ethics. First, a more traditional discussion of the issues will have to wait until later. Of course, you will read about discrimination and environmental ethics in this book, but such discussions will tend to be examples or illustrations of points rather than close examinations of topics. The advantage to studying methods first and issues second is that when you do focus on the issues, you will be better prepared, and your examination will be more productive and insightful. It is worth the wait.

Second, this book is difficult. By contrast with shallow reflection on fashionable topics in business ethics, the study of ethical methodology demands serious attention and concentration. Improved thinking in any subject does not come easily; one must pay the price. Business ethics is no different. The easy way is to discuss a case or an issue until conversation falters and then proceed to the next issue. We say, then, that we are "familiarizing" ourselves with issues in business ethics. But this is just a euphemistic excuse for failing to provide insight in a systematic way. Similarly, we could familiarize ourselves with a chemistry laboratory without learning any real chemistry. In this book, we study the "chemistry" of business ethics. In the process of doing so, we will necessarily become better acquainted with many of the topical issues as well, but the primary focus will remain on *method*.

The advantages of a methodological approach to business ethics are, by now, obvious. It provides training that should extend far beyond the pages of this book. It is skills oriented. It promotes *better* thinking about business ethics, not just *more* thinking. It measures its success in terms of insights achieved beyond this book, not just familiarization with the issues at hand. It equips the serious student of business ethics with the tools for continued and improved observation and analysis.

A second and more subtle advantage of the methodological approach, which will be apparent only to persons already familiar with professional literature in the field, is its ability to provide a unifying foundation that is largely absent from self-contained examinations of issues in business ethics. When approached from a topical perspective, business ethics issues turn on different themes. One issue, like advertising ethics, is a function of what we mean by deception; another issue, like discrimination, relates to questions of fairness and the conflict of rights; yet another issue, like environmental ethics, turns on the relative importance of different human values. And so on. Each issue seems to be considered in isolation; no transferable wisdom is accumulated in shifting from one issue to another. But using the methodological approach, the hope for a more unified perspective increases. The tendency toward fragmentation of issues in business ethics is dampened by the necessity of employing the same basic method in considering all issues.

Review of the Chapters

The main message of this book is that administrative decision making proceeds simultaneously according to two sets of criteria, which will be outlined in *Chapter Two*: utilitarianism and formalism. The purpose of the remaining chapters is to clarify these two methods and to illustrate their use.

The first task will be to trace the historical and philosophical foundations of the two main ethical methodologies, formalism and utilitarianism. This is the purpose of *Chapter Three*. Here these two theories are outlined, and biographical sketches of their founders are presented.

Historically, however, formalism and utilitarianism have played the role of antagonists. In searching for a method for making ethical decisions, we assume that we are looking for one method, not two; finding two, we naturally assume that one is an imposter. For many decades, proponents of both views have battled each other to secure the high ground in the debate over which method best represents moral judgment. The purpose of *Chapter Four*, however, is to deny that there is one true method in ethics and to assert the complementarity of formalism and utilitarianism.

Once the legitimacy of both views is established and their respective moral domains are indicated, we can take a closer look at each decision-making method. *Chapter Five* focuses on utilitarianism, especially in its managerial setting. What it finds is that decisive managers do not necessarily follow the rigorous classical guidelines in making decisions of utility; instead, they often take shortcuts by identifying decisive factors. The purpose of this chapter, then, is to describe and illustrate a more decisive managerial form of utilitarian analysis.

Chapter Six turns the spotlight on formalism. Dissatisfied with the cryptic jargon of Kantian formalism, I have tried to demystify this kind of thinking. As described in this chapter, formalistic ethical reasoning consists of a reiterative interplay between case and principle. And although this process can be highly complex, at least it is clear. It is a particularly important process from the perspective of the administration of organizational policies and rules, where consistency of application and enforcement are moral requisites.

Having two methods available for making ethical decisions is awkward. The use of both methods is required to avoid the traditional contentions between formalists and utilitarians that have plagued philosophy for so many years. This is especially true for managers who must balance the influence of the two ethical criteria in the design and enforcement of organizational rules. *Chapter Seven* shows, in theory at least, how this balance is achieved.

Chapter Eight entertains the possibility that in practice the form of balancing described in Chapter Six is almost an artistic talent that is very difficult to describe. *Chapter Nine* defends the ethical perspective against its chief opponent in the world of business, namely, the idea that it is all right to play by the "rules of the game," no matter what those rules are.

Reading Tips

Although this book may be a little more difficult than the standard textbook on business ethics, there are a couple of helpful features that may facilitate its reading. First, at the end of each chapter is a "Summary of Key Concepts" that serves as an outline of the most important points in the chapter. Two or three of the chapters are rather complex, and a short list of the main ideas may help to place the material in perspective and enable one to perceive the essence of the chapter without being overwhelmed by the size or complexity of the argument. Of course, if I were reading a good mystery, I would not recommend turning to the last page; but this book is not a novel, and reading the summary at the end of each chapter is not evidence of intellectual incontinence. On the contrary, like a table of contents, the summaries may provide a quick overview that will facilitate a closer, more successful reading of the material.

Second, the exercises and questions at the end of each chapter are an integral part of the book. They provide much evidence of the practical application of the ideas and theories developed in each chapter. To skip the exercises and questions may give the reader an impression that this book is good for theory but will not work in practice. So, at least look over the questions.

Last, don't forget to take the diagnostic test in the Appendix of this book. It will help you to determine what kind of ethical person you are. If possible, wait until Chapter Three to take the test; it will be most relevant and meaningful at that point.

C H A P T E R

2

The Three Languages of Ethics

Ethics is a matter of both the heart and the head, and people can do right or wrong things for either reason. If our hearts are set on improper satisfactions, if our desires and preferences are maladjusted, we may make ethical mistakes; likewise, we can blunder if we fail to think clearly about our choices and situations.

The connection of the heart to business activity has long been an issue. There is little agreement on the nature of the profit motive, and opinions on its nature range from pure greed to patriotic service. Indeed, one of the most needed ethical contributions in business is a determination of the essential nature of business activity. Is "doing business" something ennobling, as argued, for example, by Michael Novak in his book *The Spirit of Democratic Capitalism*?[1] Or are the Marxists correct in asserting that the concern over business ethics is just a veneer covering a societal pathology that degrades important elements of human nature?

Important as this topic is, this book chooses to attend to the other half of the business ethics issue, namely, matters of the head. Confused thinking in ethics is as common as flawed motives, but it may be an easier defect to cure. In a liberal society such as ours, telling people how they ought to *feel* about matters is generally regarded as purely relative. Within the broad constraints of the law, Americans generally reach

11

their own conclusions. But telling people how they ought to *think* is more accepted. In fact, as William Barrett has argued, the Western world in the twentieth century has come to worship technique or method.[2] We may not solve all our problems, but we think they can be solved if we hit upon the right method or procedure (something like the racetrack attitude, where successful bettors are suspected of having a system when in fact they are just lucky).

So, business people feel more comfortable discussing methods or ideas than motives or feelings. And even though a more substantial contribution to business ethics might be made by an insightful analysis of feelings and motives in business, the preponderance of poor *thinking* in ethics is ample justification for the present work.

Doing, Being, and Knowing:
Three Ways to Talk About Business Ethics

The purpose of this book, then, is restricted basically to examining business ethics from the standpoint of thoughts rather than feelings. This perspective will seem too restrictive to some; indeed, Chapter Eight calls attention to some of the dangers of excessive focus in the study of business ethics.

But the focus of this book is even more restrictive. For within the scope of ethics as a mental process, at least three fields of inquiry are possible. One modern philosopher, Ludwig Wittgenstein,[3] calls such fields of inquiry *language games*, indicating that each field has its own self-contained way of talking about ethics. Consequently, I argue that there are at least three "languages" in the study of business ethics. They reflect three different approaches that human beings can take toward business activity: doing, being, and knowing. As we shall see, each perspective is very different from every other. Reviewing the three languages will help us to see which is most relevant for the practice of business management and, therefore, which is to become the focus of the rest of this book. It will also be helpful to remember that ethics is not the exclusive domain of any particular language or perspective and that business ethics, in the end, must give appropriate recognition to all three.

Doing What's Right: The Language of Behavioral Science

The first language of business ethics is basically the language of those who do empirical research in human behavior and its causes. A scientific approach to ethics will typically assume that behavior is the result of certain casual factors — physiological, sociological, or psychological. Some of the business ethics research done in the past decade tried to impose such causal models on behavior in organizations, looking for explanations or causes of behavior that informed administrators might be able to manipulate for organizational or other goals. Causes can be almost anything: religious, cultural, and personal values, organizational goals or policies, professional codes, individual attributes such as psychological characteristics, one's position, self-concept, various demographic factors, and so on. Studies of organizational ethics often draw heavily upon work done in adjacent fields, such as social psychology or industrial psychology.

Studies in Moral Development One series of empirical studies of moral behavior was initiated by the work of Lawrence Kohlberg, a psychologist, who developed a theory of moral developmental stages experienced sequentially by individuals in the maturation process. Briefly, those stages are as follows:

Stage 1: Punishment and obedience

Stage 2: Self-gratification

Stage 3: Approval of others

Stage 4: Law and order

Stage 5: Social contract

Stage 6: Universal ethical principles

We won't take the time to examine his theory more closely here, but the basic ideas are fairly intuitive. According to

13

Kohlberg, these stages range from connecting right and wrong to punishments and rewards to thinking of right and wrong in terms of moral principles. Assuming that the level of moral development is reflected in differences in behavior, several researchers have studied the correlation between individual behavior and the level of moral development. One of Kohlberg's studies confirmed the hypothesis that principled people are less likely to obey a command to harm someone else than people who have experienced less moral development.[4] Subsequent studies have shown that higher-stage subjects are less likely to cheat on exams,[5] are more likely to assist someone in distress despite instructions to the contrary from an authority,[6] and are more likely to honor commitments.[7] A recent study proposes that Kohlberg's model of moral development can be used extensively to study moral development and ethical decision making in organizations.[8]

Influence of the Situation   One of the causal factors of most interest in the study of business ethics is the *situation, or context of action*. Much unethical behavior in organizational life can be attributed to the strength of the situation in overriding whatever individual attributes might dictate otherwise. For example, accepting bribes, selling morally repugnant products ranging from cigarettes to military arms, and deceptive accounting on government contracts can often be attributed to the compelling nature of the situation. A typical excuse for such behavior is, "If we don't, somebody else will." Restraints placed on American business behavior overseas by the Foreign Corrupt Practices Act are also thought to place American businesses in a very difficult and uncompetitive position. Again, American businesses reply, "If we don't, somebody else will."

Some of the most interesting studies of situational influences upon individual ethical behavior were conducted in the 1970s by social psychologists. Stanley Milgram's obedience study[9] was the first of these, but it was soon followed by a series of experiments investigating the effect of situation upon behavior. In one study,[10] seminary students (with the highest expressed standards of moral behavior) exhibited behavior that contradicted their expressed values. The situation was this: Each of 40 students was told to prepare and deliver a lecture on one of two topics—the parable of the Good Samaritan or job opportunities for graduates. Half of the students in each group were told that they had ample time to prepare, while the other half were told that they must hurry. On the way to the lecture location, each student passed a man in distress (actually an actor). Of the 40 subjects, only 16 stopped to help him, and most of those were from the group that thought they had plenty of time to get to the lecture. Surprisingly, the title of their assigned lecture had no bearing on their willingness to stop to help another person in need. Obviously, the pressure of the situation compelled even seminary students who had just prepared notes on the parable of the Good Samaritan to act contrary to fundamental values espoused by their religion. If seminary students can be so distracted from morally responsive behavior by a compelling situation, can business persons be any more likely to survive difficult situations morally intact?

A second astonishing study was conducted by Phillip Zimbardo and his associates in 1973.[11] Remodeling the basement of the Stanford University psychology building to resemble a prison, the researchers selected twenty-four subjects to play the roles of prisoners and guards for 2 weeks. (The subjects were selected on the basis of psychological tests that showed them to be normal average persons.) Guards were dressed up in appropriate uniforms, complete with silvered glasses and nightsticks, and prisoners were minimally dressed in smocks, with a tight cap on their heads to simulate shaven heads. Although the shared understanding was that this was an experiment and that no one would be physically mistreated or abused, the experiment lasted for only 6 days. Several prisoners developed symptoms of severe psychological stress, while the guards tended to enjoy and even exploit their acquired power and authority. In short, because of the structure of the situation, prisoners and guards began to act out their roles too realistically, and the experiment had to be terminated more than a week early in order to avoid psychological trauma to the volunteer participants.

The implications of such experiments for business ethics are enormous. If the strongest values of ordinary people can be subverted by the compulsions inherent in situations of

15

haste or of the distribution of power, what can happen to business persons whose normal daily routines embody the pressure of deadlines and differences of authority and power? Although, on the surface, business scandals might be attributed to a person's greed or selfishness, a more scientifically interesting explanation would focus on the situation for causes that might apply to human beings in general in that situation. Where such causes can be found, we tend to blame not primarily the persons but rather the situation, which we come to see as causing or contributing to the problems. Thus, from a scientific perspective, designing organizations in terms of the distribution of power, authority, and various pressures raises important ethical issues.

In response to such pressures, both from within and without the organization, business managers can take a variety of steps to prevent their organizations from feeling like "prisons":

1. They can adopt and enforce ethical codes.
2. They can create "watchdog" positions, such as that of ombudsman, to accept complaints and concerns from employees.
3. They can design internal accounting and reporting systems to discourage manipulation of company documents and records.
4. They can treat employees fairly when making hiring, promotion, and training decisions.
5. In general, they can create a corporate culture of openness and cooperation.

All of these practices tend to promote an environment that is less dehumanizing and more consistent with human ethical needs than are sometimes found in organizations. And the scientific study of the factors in organizations that enhance or distort human values and behavior is the primary source of such improved understanding.

So, the scientific study of behavior in organizations is one legitimate and important way of approaching the study of business ethics. Its strength lies in its ability to identify the factors that influence behavior, but its weakness consists of an inability to prescribe. That is, the scientific study of organizational behavior may tell us what causes result in certain kinds of behavior, but, strictly speaking, it cannot tell us what ought or ought not to be done. Scientists describe the world; they leave it up to us to decide what to do with the information they provide. A scientist who gives an opinion about what ought to be done in some situation gives a *personal* opinion only; as a *scientist*, he or she remains silent concerning matters of preference or policy.

So, other languages for thinking about business ethics become appropriate in order to provide the normative or prescriptive content not supplied by scientific research. The second language of business ethics responds to these needs — human virtues.

Being Right: The Language of the Virtues

More than 2,000 years ago, Aristotle gave an account of ethics that consisted of an analysis of the virtues. For 1,800 years or so, scholarly ethical inquiry (apart from religious doctrine) consisted of an examination of the virtues and their application to human living. Not until the work of Martin Luther and Thomas Hobbes did the modern world repudiate the classical view of human nature.[12]

Aristotle taught that human beings have a specific nature, with certain aims and goals, and that the possession of the virtues was what enabled individuals to realize their full human natures. The ultimate good life toward which human beings strive was called by Aristotle *eudaimonia*, which means something like blessedness, happiness, or prosperity. The strength of Aristotle's account of ethics lies in its recognition of human agency or responsibility for action. That is, people are both praised and blamed for what they do, which exhibits the presence or absence of virtues — unlike the later scientific approach, which makes no normative judgments but simply identifies and describes internal and external causes and associations.

In the world of business, where leadership is highly valued and is allegedly taught at major universities, the language of

17

virtue has great appeal for accounting for ethical (or at least successful) behavior. We describe business leaders, for example, in the following ways:

ambitious	avaricious
courageous	dictatorial
disciplined	impulsive
persistent	secretive
prudent	threatening
reasonable	vengeful

The existence of a language of virtues reminds us that there is also a language of vices. Using such language efficiently conveys a basic acquaintance with a person and characterizes him or her as prone to certain forms of ethical or unethical behavior. Such qualities are also extremely useful for describing individual instances of behavior.

Despite its usefulness, however, the language of virtues has been ignored in the field of business ethics, except for journalistic or casual forms of exposition in the media. This is due to at least a couple of historical factors. First, throughout the centuries, merchants were generally regarded as less virtuous than other persons. Although merchants were thought of as industrious and prudent, they were also described as acquisitive, deceitful, selfish, and exploitative. Thus, an open discussion of the virtues as applied to business behavior was not promoted by people in business.

Second, there are academic reasons for the historical absence of the virtues in scholarly accounts of business activity. Accounts of business success point as often to vices as to virtues. Popular television shows like "Dallas" seem to imply that business success depends on personal vices. But this is hardly a modern idea. Three hundred years ago, Bernard Mandeville's "The Grumbling Hive" argued, for example, that thriving economic systems are maintained in part by private vices. This theme was echoed somewhat by Adam Smith, who identified "self-love" (or the pursuit of one's own interests as opposed to others') as the major cause of the national accumulation of wealth. This general theme of private vices and public virtues is generally supported by modern Western economists, including such well-known persons as Milton Friedman. As a result, such individual virtues as cooperation, generosity, benevolence, and civility (to name a few) are seldom used to characterize the required virtues attending modern business success. Consequently, the language of virtues has not appealed to business scholars, who generally espouse the profit motive, which in turn is described more easily in terms of vices than virtues.

Despite these natural antagonisms, however, interest in the language of the virtues has recently been renewed. This revival of the virtues is not promoted by business scholars, however; it comes from philosophers who are frustrated by the narrow scope of ethical theory and recognize in the language of the virtues a richness that more fully comprehends the range of human ethical behavior. Alasdair MacIntyre, for example, defends the classical account of the virtues in *After Virtue*,[13] and Edmund Pincoffs echoes this general theme in his *Quandaries and Virtues: Against Reductivism in Ethics*.[14] These recent books are important contributions to the field and challenge business scholars to rethink the usual ways of teaching business ethics.

Increased attention to the language of the virtues may prove very productive in business ethics for two reasons. First, it will broaden the scope of ethical inquiry to include forms of behavior only obliquely referred to heretofore as matters of management style or personality. For example, Pascale and Athos,[15] the authors of *The Art of Japanese Management,* describe Japanese management in terms of some nonclassical virtues: what the authors refer to as *going with the flow, balancing, indirection,* and so on. They even employ some Japanese terms to try to indicate some managerial characteristics that they feel are important for superior managerial behavior. So, by employing the language of virtues to describe managerial behavior, the range of ethical behavior is significantly broadened beyond the scope of policy making and decision making.

Second, the language of virtues will focus attention on the connection between business activity and human maturation or flourishing. We may legitimately ask, for example, does a particular form of business activity (say, cigarette manufacturing and distribution) promote human virtue? Do state lotteries

19

promote richness of human living or just produce lucky winners? In a liberal society such as ours, where all activities not prohibited by law are allowed and even defended under the banner of liberalism and freedom, an enhanced ability to discuss the relation of business activity to human development may help us to be more ethically discriminating in our choices while still tolerating the freedom granted to all to pursue their own ends. That is, without making a legal or political judgment about a firm's right to do business, we may nevertheless legitimately judge a firm's contribution to human virtue or vice and to our own personal well-being.

A general theory of human virtue as applied to business activity would be a major ethical accomplishment indeed; at this point, no such theory exists. Perhaps the chief obstacles in the way of such a contribution are the individualism and general freedom of thought that permeate our national values, which would criticize such a project in terms of its subjectivity. A more objective approach to ethics has generally been accepted in recent years among management scholars. This is the language of ethical theory, as grounded in the philosophical ethicism of the nineteenth century. It is to this language that we now give attention.

Knowing What's Right: The Language of Ethical Theory

Ethical theory has been the preferred language of management ethics for several years. This connection is the result of several interesting historical circumstances. First, in the post-Watergate era, as authors became more and more interested in giving ethics serious treatment in schools of business, a very willing source of help was available in departments of philosophy. And since the dominant language of ethics in philosophy for the last 200 years has been ethical theory, the transfer of ethical theory to business ethics textbooks was natural. Second, ethical theory traditionally consists of a classical duality represented by utilitarianism and formalism, both claiming to be decision procedures in ethics. Given the natural interest of business managers in the techniques of decision making, characterizing business ethics as chiefly a matter of executive decision making seemed appropriate. Furthermore, one of the classical approaches—utilitarianism—has strong affinities with other deeply rooted business decision-making techniques, such as cost-benefit analysis and decision theory. Business administrators already spoke the language of ethical theory; they merely needed to have their outlook broadened and their vocabulary enhanced. So, for good reasons, ethical theory has been the dominant model of ethical inquiry in business ethics in recent decades.

Although ethical theory will be discussed in considerable detail in subsequent chapters, a simple description is this: Ethical theory is the systematic study of procedures for deciding on the right course of action in any given situation. As suggested previously, ethical theory is not unitary; it is most often described as consisting of two—and sometimes three or more—ways of making decisions about ethical issues. Traditionally, the dominant perspectives are utilitarianism and formalism. The basis of utilitarianism is the idea that that which is right is that which brings about the best overall results—a very simple idea that becomes very complex in practice. Formalism, by contrast, is much harder to define. Basically, it consists of selecting the right course of action on the basis of that which most closely conforms to impartial rules or principles of action. Thus, ethics is simultaneously concerned with rules and results.

Without going into detail here about either of these views, we can provide many examples of their influence in our lives. Utilitarian thinking is found in such diverse phenomena as the following:

1. Cost-benefit analysis
2. Environmental impact studies
3. The majority vote
4. Product comparisons for consumer information
5. Tax laws
6. Consumer behavior in the free market

This list is just a beginning, but it serves to illustrate the point that utilitarian activity is found in large issues and small, abstract and concrete, public and private. In all cases, the aim is to secure the best possible results.

Formalistic thinking, by contrast, is more concerned with standardizing behavior through rules. Examples of its use include the following:

1. Wearing uniforms
2. Establishing hours of operation
3. The nonexistence of a market in human babies
4. Constitutional rights
5. Notions of fairness regarding the distribution of wealth
6. Religious doctrine

Of course, rules per se do not make just anything ethical, but the attempt to generate a total set of rules or expectations that seem to preserve important relations and values is a significantly different way of approaching ethical issues. Thus, both utilitarianism and formalism are important influences in Western culture.

Both formalist and utilitarian approaches to ethical decision making have their points of vulnerability; they will be discussed in the next chapter. But ethical theory in general also has its critics. One writer, Edmund Pincoffs, describes the traditional ethical theoretic orientation as *quandary ethics* and outlines four essential characteristics of this view that he finds troubling:

1. *It is situational.* That is, its context is disputation, deliberation, and justification, to the exclusion of questions of moral character. It begins with a problem and seeks a solution.
2. *The situations are described in general terms.* Idiosyncratic details are morally unimportant for this orientation. Using case studies to demonstrate the application of ethical theory is a good example of generality.
3. *No reference is made to the decision maker as an individual with distinctive characteristics.* Ethics is not a matter of style or personality or individual capabilities;

it is a function of the situation. The right thing to do is still right, whether or not an individual possesses certain traits that facilitate or impede the performance of the action.

4. ***Resolution of the problem is confined to the conscientiousness of the agent—what Pincoffs also calls* rule responsibility**. Such rules may be rules of thumb or more absolute rules, but quandary ethics requires respect for the general determinations of the methods from case to case.[16]

To illustrate these aspects of ethical theoretic analysis, let's look at a simple, but typical, case. Suppose the project leader of an engineering team has been approached by his supervisor and told to charge the time on a recent job to another "fatter" government contract. The work was necessary, the price charged was fair, and the government is paying in either case. The project leader knows that he would jeopardize his job by refusing to follow his supervisor's instructions, but he also knows that such behavior violates sound accounting practices and is against the law. What does he do?

1. This case illustrates a problem; it is situational.
2. The case is described in very general terms. In fact, it is essentially similar to countless other cases like it in which personal conscience conflicts with organizational demands.
3. We know nothing about the individual characteristics of the project leader.
4. Resolution of the case turns on a common dilemma: Should one be loyal to organizational interests and practices, or should one obey the law?

For Pincoffs, these characteristics represent criticisms of the ethical theoretic approach because they reduce excessively the scope of ethical discussion. What we find in such a case is the ethical theoretic "bones"; what is ignored, according to Pincoffs, is the "flesh" of ethics—individual personalities, virtues

23

other than conscientiousness, all that confers novelty and uniqueness upon individual experience. And although Chapter Seven of this book largely agrees with Pincoffs's criticisms, such criticisms are more like finishing touches than fundamental flaws. Where the professional lives of business managers are concerned, ethical theory is highly relevant and not to be taken lightly. Managers work constantly in an environment that demands just such an approach. They adopt general policies and administer general rules; they respond to various groups pressing for reasons or justifications for many different actions and decisions; and in general, they defend, explain, account for, deliberate, and decide. The array of tasks facing managers is well matched to ethical theory. *It may be nice for a manager to have virtues, but it is imperative for a manager to have reasons.*

Therefore, the dominant ethical language of management is the language of ethical justification, or ethical theory. And good administrators should be prepared to pursue all three approaches where necessary: science, the virtues, and ethical theory. Furthermore, the three languages of ethics outlined here are not meant to exhaust the possibilities. One important ethical language not examined here is *religion*. It may indeed be that in the end the most important language of ethical administration is religious. But that possibility would seem to require greater homogeneity of belief than is typically found in Western business organizations. So, from a practical perspective, we must leave that discussion for another time.

An Illustration of the Three Languages

To illustrate the use of the three languages of ethics in business management, an example is helpful. However, the choice of an example itself depends upon the language employed, because the way the issue is presented already implies the influence of some particular language. Keeping this difficulty in mind, we will examine the following case taken from *The Art of Japanese Management*, by Pascale and Athos, in terms of the different orientations of each of these languages.[17] The case is realistic enough to invite comment under each of the languages of ethics.

At 8:04 A.M., the intercom bleeped.

"Mr. Kemper," said the secretary in a lowered voice, "there are four cabin cleaners in reception — blacks — and they insist on seeing you. They seem angry." Mr. Kemper paused, drumming his fingers on the stacks of papers that had brought him to work an hour early, before his day of nonstop meetings began. "Sounds like one we'd better deal with," he replied. "Send them in." For Larry T. Kemper, regional manager of United Airlines, overseer of 20,000 employees in the western United States, and eight organizational levels removed from the hourly cabin cleaners he was about to encounter, the day had begun. Cabin cleaners are among the lowest paid and least skilled airline employees. Their occupation involves hours of waiting, punctuated by frenzied bursts of activity when, working on tight turnaround schedules, they pour through the planes, cleaning out seat pockets, ashtrays, galleys, and restrooms. The grievance that the contingent wished to communicate was that their white foreman consistently assigned them the most unpleasant jobs. They wanted him to change that.

The challenge for Mr. Kemper was manifold. As a senior manager in a firm priding itself on its open-door policy, he sought to reaffirm the company commitment to having all levels of management open to communication from below. Moreover, the problem had clear racial overtones, which he needed to grasp and defuse lest the issue mushroom into something larger. Furthermore, he needed to conduct himself so as not to undercut the seven levels of management between himself and the supervisor of the aggrieved cleaners. Finally, there was a union issue. Although members of the airline mechanics union, the cleaners had chosen an independent channel outside the traditional grievance machinery. The problem had to be handled in such a way as not to offend the union or set precedents that would bring an avalanche of such grievances to Mr. Kemper's desk.

From the perspective of *ethical theory*, the situation is appropriate because it represents a particular quandary or situation that needs to be resolved. A variety of questions comes to mind:

What are Mr. Kemper's alternatives?

Doing what would bring about the most good?

What precedent would he be setting?

Are there any applicable company policies?

What results does he wish to achieve?

What company, union, and personal rules or policies are in conflict, and how can that conflict be resolved?

Can correct behavior be identified in terms of a rule or policy for future use in similar situations?

From the perspective of the *virtues*, the case is more of an illustrative story (as Pascale and Athos have used it) than a situation that needs to be resolved. Pascale and Athos use the case to illustrate a particular managerial virtue that they variously refer to as *juggling, balancing, going with the flow*, and in other terms. The purpose of doing ethics is the inculcation of virtue, not the resolution of a particular problem. Therefore, cases serve as stories, illustrations, or even myths, by contrast with their function in the language of ethical theory.

From the *scientific* perspective, we are looking for interesting phenomena and their general causes. For example, we might hypothesize that the conflict arose from the structure of organizational relationships, or from the distribution of power, or from a particular management style, or from the personality traits of the individuals involved, including a variety of other factors in various combinations. Scientists would also be interested in discovering the best management approach to use in disarming and resolving situations like this one. They might investigate such matters in a real business setting through the use of observation or questionnaires, or in a controlled laboratory experimental simulation, or in an experimental design on site.

So, there are at least three legitimate ways to think about what is right. Each has its own language, and each contributes in its own way to a fuller understanding of correct behavior. From the managerial perspective, however, the dominant ethical language is the perspective of ethical theory, since it is the language of ethical justification. And giving reasons or accounting for behavior is a managerial necessity.

The Myth of Either-Or Managing

Having identified the focus of managerial ethics to be ethical theory, we can now make a few general observations to prepare us for what follows. First, although ethical decision making is often described as a choice between right and wrong, this either-or dichotomy is rather misleading. It is often more accurate to say that managerial ethics represents a choice between better and best or between two kinds of right, namely, the utilitarian right and the formalistic right. The "right versus wrong" model is a popular one, promoted by the mass media. This polarized way of thinking is illustrated by other related pairs of concepts, such as guilt and innocence, truth and falsehood, good and bad results, open discussions and cover-ups, and so on.

But when this highly constraining model of right versus wrong is employed, several kinds of frustrations are likely to occur. Aware of the great subtleties in decision making, *managers* feel boxed in or misunderstood by a general public looking for a yes-or-no decision—they expect either this or that. And intuitively sensing that decisions are more often choices among multiple rights or goods, managers may develop a disdain of or disrespect for the law, which often is formulated in terms of dos and don'ts. *Students*, likewise, become frustrated with the subtle differences between one choice and another and, mistakenly supposing that such choices represent right and wrong, they conclude that there are no answers in ethics. Therefore, they adopt an ethically relativistic position or lose all interest in ethics. As Alfred North Whitehead said, "The simple minded use of the notions 'right' and 'wrong' is one of the chief obstacles to the progress of understanding."[18]

These frustrations and ensuing mistakes are due to a defective way of thinking about ethics that is too impatient, too simple, and too unforgiving. Ethical decisions, especially for administrators, are seldom choices between right and wrong; they are more often choices between two kinds of right. This is due to various factors, all of which relate to the duality in ethical theory represented by utilitarianism and formalism.

First, from a utilitarian point of view, because *right* refers to the optimal choice among several alternatives for action, *wrong* can refer to any other choice, including some that may be almost as good as the optimal choice. For example, a manager choosing from among several proposals for community involvement, from a utilitarian perspective, would attempt to select the proposal that would simply bring about the most good. But supposing the less than optimal proposals to be wrong ignores a wide variety of possible behavior that is much worse, including lack of community involvement or even alternatives that would antagonize the community. In such a decision situation, it would be more appropriate to say that the manager is selecting from among multiple right choices than it would be to say that the manager is choosing between right and wrong.

From the formalistic perspective, the choice between two rights is easily illustrated by the common difficulty of knowing which of two or more ethical principles to apply to a given case. Should one be totally honest, even if it means hurting someone's feelings? So, formalistic analysis often presents the decision maker with a choice between two rights and not just between a right and a wrong.

Second, and more important, utilitarian and formalistic analyses sometimes appear to diverge in their recommendations for action. This is not evidence that ethical theory is faulty; rather, it indicates that ethical behavior is often a delicate balancing of equally legitimate "pulls" in ethics. A more detailed discussion follows in Chapters Four and Seven, but a simple example can be given here. Think for a minute of the way the game of professional baseball is constructed. Defensively, baseball is organized on utilitarian grounds: Each player is selected for a position in accordance with the skills he or she displays. Those who can catch grounders and can throw accurately off balance, for example, are assigned to the infield; those who can run fast, catch fly balls, and throw hard play the outfield; those who have special pitching skills become pitchers; and so forth. From the defensive perspective, *the team gets the best results* by placing each available player in his or her optimally contributing position.

From the offensive perspective, however, baseball is organized formalistically. Although the same players may be assigned to bat first or last in the lineup, *the same rule applies to all*, including the pitcher: All players bat. This is a formalistic approach in the sense that all players are treated the same way. Its ethical purpose is similar to that of rotating players equally from position to position, as in volleyball. By contrast, a utilitarian approach to offense in baseball might be quite different and would certainly get far better results. For example, instead of requiring each player to bat, one might select only the best three or four hitters from among those playing, or platoon offensive and defensive teams, selecting batters from among those not playing defense, and so on. Indeed, there might be many ways to get better offensive results in baseball other than simply requiring all players to bat, but the balance of defensive utility with offensive "universality" (or equality) represents two essential features of team sports: getting the greatest contribution from each player and treating each player as a full and equal member of the team.

By analogy, the same is true in ethics in general. Business administrators must balance the pulls of equality and efficiency, of rules and results. But they cannot always do so simultaneously. Sometimes rules are set aside to secure exceptional results; at other times, promising alternatives may be overruled by organizational policy or by local, state, or federal law. So, choices in many situations will represent a choice between two or more rights rather than a choice between right and wrong.

Ethically speaking, administrators are in a difficult position. This doesn't mean that they are compelled by insidious organizational factors to behave immorally; they are no more or less moral than any other person. Rather, it means that they are at the center of responsibility in our society for ethical behavior in public and private institutions. Administrators not only need to decide what is correct behavior, they need to *explain* those decisions to a public that speaks a variety of ethical languages and is reluctant to entertain all but the simplest explanations in any language.

So, in what follows, we take seriously the injunction that good thinking in ethics is a skill that is critical for successful management and, like many other skills, can be improved with study. This, in turn, implies a kind of classical realism in ethics, namely, that what ought to be done in a given situation is discovered or realized as an objectively ascertainable prescription. Were this not true, administrators would simply be cultural technicians, playing at administration according to the rules of a game but having no particular relation to human nature. However, there is an objective component in ethics. Whether this makes the task of the administrator easier or harder is debatable. Were there no objective component to ethics, reasonability would reduce to mere persuasion; and some may think that persuading others is easier than reasoning with them, at least in the short term.

So, the administrator is at the center of responsibility in organizational life. The task of being ethically reasonable may not be easy, but this book assumes that it is worth the effort. Learning to think well in ethics is as important as having the right feelings about things, and it may be an easier quality to acquire. Many administrators possess this quality already; what this book tries to do is to describe what successful administrators do. This is less of an academic exercise than a practical survey, but it is at least a little of both. Careful thinking should produce improved results, and the following chapters have been written with just such a goal in mind.

Summary of Key Concepts

1. Business ethics can be approached legitimately from the standpoint of either one's thoughts or one's feelings. The purpose of this book is to do the former: learn how to *think* better on ethical issues.

2. When thinking about ethics, at least three legitimate approaches come to mind:
    a. Behavioral science
    b. Virtues
    c. Ethical theory

3. The ethical concern of some behavioral sciences is to understand what influences persons to perform actions that we judge to be unethical. Examples of such studies include:
    a. Lawrence Kohlberg's study of moral development
    b. Darley and Batson's study of seminary students under stress
    c. Zimbardo's simulation of a prison environment
    Through such studies, scientists learn more about what causes people to behave the way they do, especially in ethical situations.

4. A second way of dicussing ethics is to focus on individuals' *character* traits as things worthy of our emulation. This is the language of *virtues*. Aristotle laid the groundwork for this approach more than 2,000 years ago.

5. The language of virtues has not been popular in the business world, at least in this century. Moreover, this focus disappeared far earlier in the field of philosophy, displaced by rising interest in ethical theory. However, despite its disuse in business ethics, the language of virtues is becoming increasingly important for establishing personal values with respect to business activity.

6. A third approach is the language of ethical theory, which consists of two sophisticated and well-developed positions: utilitarianism, which focuses on *results*, and formalism, which focuses on *rules*.

7. Ethical theory sees ethical situations neither as determined by causes nor as occasions for virtue, but rather as quandaries to be resolved. This may be a narrow perspective on ethics, but it is important for the modern administrator.

8. A clearer understanding of ethical theory can show us how either-or thinking in ethics is too simple. Managers often choose from among two or more rights, not between a right and a wrong.

Questions and Exercises

1. List six or eight team sports, and reflect upon whether the rules of competition are modeled after utilitarian or formalistic requirements.

2. Benjamin Franklin's autobiography lists the following virtues, which he thought were important for human moral development: temperance, silence, order, resolution, frugality, industry, sincerity, justice, moderation, cleanliness, tranquility, chastity, and humility. Which ones still apply in the modern business world? Which do not? Which are missing? Has the basic character of the business person changed since Franklin's time?

3. List as quickly as possible your own business heroes or heroines. Is this easy to do? If not, what does that imply about your own motives for studying business?

4. Review recent ethics cases in the news to see if the two-rights model is more appropriate than the right-wrong model.

5. Thinking about recent ethics cases in the news, which ones seem to turn on questions of motive or virtues, as opposed to the quality of thinking?

6. Robert Fulghum wrote the following famous essay, called "All I Ever Really Needed to Know I Learned in Kindergarten." It is a good example of ethics of the heart:

> Most of what I really need to know about how to live, what to do, and how to be I learned in kindergarten. Wisdom was not at the top of the graduate school mountain, but there in the sandbox at nursery school.
>
> These are the things I learned: Share everything. Play fair. Don't hit people. Put things back where you found them. Clean up your own mess. Don't take things that aren't yours. Say you're sorry when you hurt somebody. Wash your hands before you eat. Flush. Warm milk and cookies are good for you. Live a balanced life. Learn some and think some and draw and paint and sing and dance and play and work every day some.

Take a nap every afternoon. When you go out into the world, watch for traffic, hold hands, and stick together. Be aware of wonder. Remember the little seed in the plastic cup. The roots go down and the plant goes up and nobody really knows how or why, but we are all like that. . . .

And then remember the book about Dick and Jane and the first word you learned, the biggest word of all—LOOK. Everything you need to know is in there somewhere. The Golden Rule and love and basic sanitation. Ecology and politics and sane living.

Think of what a better world it would be if we all—the whole world—had cookies and milk about three o'clock every afternoon and then lay down with our blankets for a nap. Or if we had a basic policy in our nation, and other nations, to always put things back where we found them and clean up your own messes. And it is still true, no matter how old you are, when you go out into the world, it is best to hold hands and stick together. (Robert Fulghum, *All I Really Need to Know I Learned in Kindergarten.* New York: Villard Books, a Division of Random House, Inc., 1988, pp. 6–8)

   a. Is ethics as simple as it is claimed to be here? How are these recommendations both relevant and irrelevant for today's business manager?

   b. When might "hold hands and stick together" be bad advice?

C H A P T E R

3

Two Sides to Ethical Theory

If managerial decision making is to be ethical, we must first agree on how to decide whether or not an action is ethical. Leaving ethics up to intuition, gut feelings, or office politics is not good enough for the thoughtful manager; none of these "methods" seems reliable enough to inspire confidence and ensure consistently good judgment. What is needed is some indicator or criterion that, if satisfied, guarantees ethical acceptability. For example, just as the criterion for drunk driving is a test of the level of blood alcohol, there must be some test or criterion for all forms of behavior that indicates ethical status. In this chapter we introduce that criterion for ethical action; *we decide how to decide*.

Traditionally, those who have been most interested in this issue are the philosophers. The philosophical search for an ethical criterion was begun almost single-handedly by Aristotle. His discussion of the human virtues and of the role of reason in controlling passion and desire guided philosophical ethics for almost 2,000 years.[1] In the modern era, however, the search has all but abandoned Aristotle in favor of two rival views of ethics that have greatly influenced world affairs in the twentieth century. One is ethical formalism, whose founder is Immanuel Kant. The other is utilitarianism, which was most fully developed by Jeremy Bentham. We turn first to utilitarian ethics to see what test it proposes as a criterion for moral behavior.

35

Utilitarianism: Looking for Results

Consider the following case:

Suppose a company that manufactures computer chips is considering manufacturing and marketing a new product that involves the accumulation of large amounts of hazardous waste by-products. Unfortunately, the storage site is in an industrial park in the suburbs and is too small to allow further efficient accumulation of hazardous materials. The materials can be shipped out of state to a federally approved dump site, but that alternative is very costly. Furthermore, the company has good reason to believe that its competitors have routinely avoided costly shipments by secretly dumping their waste products in local landfills, out of sight of the law. Over the years, this company has taken pride in its relationship with the community and considers following the lead of its competitors as unfortunate but perhaps unavoidable. The company employs 5,000 persons from the local community and would be forced to lay off several hundred workers if no alternative can be found to out-of-state shipping; that still might not be enough to prevent long-term damage to the company in view of its competition.

The company does own some land 5 miles from town near the city's landfill site, which is an attractive but illegal alternative. Considering this alternative, the company's managers reason this way: The company-owned site appears secure. It is in a thick bed of clay, and there is no reason to suppose that significant seepage would occur. Storage of wastes there might never be discovered. Even if it were, administrative and court delays could take almost 5 years, and the history of recent cases like this suggests that any fine or penalty imposed would be far less than the profits that can be made from production and marketing of the product. Waiting for the government to do anything takes too much time. All things considered, the company appears to have no choice but to use the secret site.

The form of reasoning used in this case is utilitarian. That is, it compares the relative merit, or utility, of various alternatives and selects the one that promises the best results. Alternatives have worth in comparison with other alternatives as means for securing the general welfare.

The thinking described in this case is merely an illustration; it may or may not be an example of *correct* utilitarian thinking. We will return to it from time to time to illustrate various features of utilitarianism, including its strengths and weaknesses. By contrast, notice how different it is from another way of thinking about the same issue:

> The company has traditionally honored the law in nurturing its relationship with the larger community. Violating the law now would be inconsistent with past behavior and with the kind of relationship it has tried to maintain. The success of this corporation and of the community is inextricably connected to the subtle forms of interdependence and mutual trust achieved by common adherence to local and federal regulations that deserve our respect. The use of a private dump site is not just illegal; it is also not the sort of action we could expect or recommend others to follow. Nor could we do this and, at the same time, maintain the standards of honesty and trust that are essential for continued civility. Therefore, we either play by the rules of the game, or we don't play at all.

This second kind of thinking about the problem is strikingly different. It selects a course of action by ascertaining whether it can be consistently undertaken as a general rule without disrupting institutions upon which its own success depends. It is not directly interested in results or in comparing alternatives; instead, it inquires whether there is something about the action itself that recommends it or disallows it, independent of the worth of other possible alternatives.

This form of thinking we will label *formalism*. Like the earlier example of utilitarian thinking, this example of formalistic reasoning is only an illustration; it may or may not be correct. We will take a closer look at it shortly. But first, let's get better acquainted with utilitarian ethics and with the man who is given credit for its initial formulation—Jeremy Bentham.

Jeremy Bentham

Jeremy Bentham (1748–1832) is widely considered the founder of utilitarian ethics. Bentham had a knack for seizing ideas that were not his own and developing them into formidable tools for social reform. At least five authors discussed the basic ideas of utilitarianism before Bentham, but it is to Bentham that credit is given for the systematic development of utilitarian thinking that has secured for it a place of importance in the history of ethical thought.[2]

Bentham was a precocious child, learning Latin grammar at the age of 4. Encouraged by his father to pursue a legal career, Bentham entered Oxford University at the age of 12 and was graduated 3 years later. Preferring a life of reflection, he never practiced law. Instead, he became the leader of a group known as the "Philosophical Radicals," which advocated legal and penal reform.

Frustrated with unreasonable British legal and penal institutions, Bentham sought major reforms, writing thousands of pages in pursuit of this goal. At the age of 83 Bentham died, leaving his body for scientific dissection to a university founded by his movement—University College, London. There, still to be seen and at his request, is Jeremy Bentham's embalmed body, dressed in his accustomed clothes and surmounted by a wax model of his head—appropriately a very nontraditional ending for this reformer, but hardly one that inspires us to look to him for the foundations of good judgment! Nevertheless, Bentham's writings have had a profound impact on Western civilization in the twentieth century, and the following discussion reviews the basic principles.

The Greatest Happiness Principle

Utilitarianism presupposes one overriding moral principle that serves as the criterion for ethical judgment, namely, the greatest good for the greatest number. This principle requires that we think not merely of ourselves in choosing courses of action, but that we act so as to maximize the amount of good done to all. In the case at the beginning of this chapter, the *greatest happiness principle* requires the company to pursue not just its own benefit but the general welfare of anyone who may have an interest in, or be affected by, the company's decisions. This might even include future generations if illegal toxic waste disposal becomes a future environmental problem.

The reason Bentham was so interested in this principle is that it provided the rationale for advocating reform of laws and institutions that protected only the traditionally preferred classes of citizens while dealing harshly with others. Tradition, he felt, often discriminated, but the greatest happiness principle did not; it gave equal weight to every individual in comparing the gains and losses resulting from policy and law. Therefore, to Jeremy Bentham, the greatest happiness principle was rational, democratic, and liberal. That is, it was the instrument by which law could rest on reason rather than on tradition; it regarded all human beings as having an equal claim to public and private goods; and it allowed all persons to specify what counted as gains and losses for themselves.

An Objective Moral Criterion: Pain and Pleasure

In order to judge the amount of happiness produced by a given alternative, some general measure of happiness must be identified. For legislators and elected politicians, for example, such a measure might be letters from citizens or even votes in an election; for an economist, happiness might be measured in terms of the gross national product or the cost of living. For Jeremy Bentham, the measure of happiness was more basic: He felt that all persons are moved to action by the attraction of pleasure and the repulsion of pain. Thus, actions are right if they tend to increase the sum total of pleasure or decrease the sum total of pain of all those affected by the action.

For example, in the toxic waste case at the beginning of this chapter, pleasure might consist, in the final analysis, of lower prices for consumers and retained jobs, while pain might be illustrated by illnesses and other hazards resulting from a damaged environment. In this, as in every utilitarian analysis, there is a trade-off in comparing the pleasures and pains associated with competing alternatives. In this case, the trade-off is between short-term economic benefits and long-term health and safety. Both are good, and each has pleasurable effects, but they may not be achieved simultaneously.

We might think of *pleasure* as being synonymous with *good, benefit, advantage,* or *happiness. Pain,* by contrast, means *bad, cost, harm,* or *disadvantage.* And the goal of utilitarian analysis is to use appropriate measures of pleasure and pain to make choices for action that will secure the greatest amount of pleasure for all concerned while minimizing the pain suffered by anyone.

Quantitative Calculations

When we try to compare one alternative with another in making decisions of utility, most of us are rather casual, being satisfied with quick mental comparisons. (Let's call this the *Baskin-Robbins approach* to utilitarianism: When you are faced with 31 flavors, you just select whatever strikes your fancy at the moment.) Bentham, however, espoused a more rigorous approach. He insisted on the quantitative measurement of pain and pleasure. After all, although less rigorous methods might select an alternative more quickly, for important problems they are not reliable enough. Especially where social institutions or national policies are concerned, a slow, costly, detailed analysis is more than compensated for by the potential benefits of selecting optimal alternatives.

Modern examples of the quantitative approach to utilitarian analysis include such things as environmental impact statements and technology impact statements. Such documents can be of book length and contain sophisticated economic and social impact studies, all done from a quantitative perspective. Large corporations, as well, perform their own versions of utilitarian analysis when making product development and marketing decisions; this is called *cost-benefit analysis.* And although its scope is often limited to the achievement of organizational purposes, it illustrates the utilitarian objective of getting to numbers on the bottom line.

If we put all of the principles of utilitarian analysis together and constructed a step-by-step method for decision making, it might look like this:

1. List all the alternatives.
2. List the criteria by which the alternatives will be assessed.
3. Rank the criteria in order of priority and assign coefficients of relative importance.
4. Assess each of the alternatives in terms of its ability to satisfy the criteria listed in step 2.
5. Select the optimal alternative.

This method may seem familiar to those acquainted with cost-benefit analysis, and it should. The structures of thinking in utilitarian ethical analysis and cost-benefit analysis are very similar. Alasdair MacIntyre, for example, drew attention to these similarities and concluded that "the utilitarian vision of the world and the bureaucratic vision of the world match each other closely."[3]

Two Examples

What has been described here seems simple, but utilitarian analysis is often all but simple. Sometimes the analysis of an issue becomes very complex, and the resolution of the issue can turn on subtle comparisons embedded deep in a rigorous analysis.

For example, one issue that is clearly utilitarian but highly complex is *pornography*. The major questions of the issue focus on the possible harm to society and individuals: Does pornography do anyone any harm? Does it cause people to commit sex crimes? Or is it just a symptom of perversion that already exists? Opponents of pornography have sought to connect the existence of pornography to certain socially undesirable consequences, such as the increasing number of sex crimes—but with little success. But the range of consequences is not exhausted with an examination of the association of criminal behavior with access to pornography; a variety of other social pathologies seem to be plausible candidates, including divorce rates, sexist attitudes toward women (both domestic and corporate), and marital infidelity. However, such phenomena are difficult to study. For one thing, it's hard to know who has access to pornographic materials and who has been unfaithful in marriage. The topic demands utilitarian resolution, but it resists quantitative investigation.

A second general set of issues that connects public policy and business with utilitarian analysis is the *legalization of behaviors or products that are traditionally illegal*. More specifically, for example, several states have legalized gambling and placed it under state control. The usual rationale for such legislation is utilitarian: increased revenues, a stronger economy, more jobs, and so on. Needless to say, the opposition points to adverse consequences, such as increased criminal activity, new addictions, and broken lives. The issue is decided state by state as the examination of the consequences of such a policy recommends rejection or adoption.

Strengths and Weaknesses

Many public policy issues relating to the business world are discussed in utilitarian terms. Indeed, utilitarian analysis is often a necessity if deliberation on some issues is to be productive.

Probably the greatest strength of utilitarian analysis is its *liberality*. That is, although an omniscient and benevolent observer might make infallible judgments about what is in the best interest of those observed (or at least what should be in their best interest), few of us feel comfortable making such judgments for other adults. We judge what is in our own best interest and allow others to do the same. We allow this even when we know that the consequences of another person's behavior will be harmful to that person, such as decisions to gamble, to smoke, and to drink alcohol excessively. (Sometimes these are called *victimless crimes*.) Generally, we resist the temptation to make assumptions about what everyone ought to regard as pleasurable or harmful.

Therefore, utilitarian thinking is liberal in the classical sense: It emphasizes broad-minded and tolerant thinking and appeals to no authority in resolving differences of opinion. In theory, personal preferences are given, and homogeneity of opinion is not necessary to achieve the greatest good for the greatest number. (Remember, the greatest good for the greatest number doesn't even require consent of the majority to satisfy its demands, as long as a greater good can be achieved in no other way!) Obviously, the resolution of many social quandaries would satisfy more people if all people thought alike. And general agreement certainly simplifies utilitarian analysis. However, group thinking does not guarantee good thinking. And whether people's preferences are well considered or not, the principle of utility can still select the best option, given the circumstances, even though better options might be available if people were to change their preferences.

A second strength of utilitarian analysis is its *ability to describe* much of human decision making. Human beings make decisions of utility regularly, and the processes they use often resemble the formal steps outlined earlier: We brainstorm alternatives, gather criteria, weigh them, and assess alternatives. This theory of decision making may be more descriptive of our mental processes in selecting a new automobile than in selecting a spouse, but it undeniably describes many of our deliberations.

Utilitarianism also has inherent weaknesses. One of these is the *possibility of injustice* regarding the distribution of goods. The problem of justice is well illustrated by a short story by Ursula LeGuin called "The Ones Who Walk Away from Omelas."[4] In this story, the author has imagined a world blessed (or cursed) with almost perfect utilitarian goodness: It is a happy world for everyone, although it is happy in many different ways, varying according to the ideals of happiness for each person. The only condition of the continuing happiness of this individually ideal world is that one 9-year-old child be maintained in a mop closet in constant misery. The child blubbers, and people are moved to help the child; but no one can, since this is the one condition upon which the entire society remains happy. Tours are held to be sure that the child is still there, and from time to time visitors simply walk away from their perfect happiness — no crying, no raging; they simply walk out of the city and never return.

This story is typical of dozens of cases that are designed to illustrate the problem of justice. For the utilitarian, the thorn in the story is the realization that the highest total level of good or happiness may rest on an unwilling sacrificial lamb— for those who walk away from Omelas, an apparently repugnant moral circumstance. But the problem is not for the utilitarian alone; the formalist is made nervous by this story as well, since although taking the child out of the mop closet treats all persons equally and with respect, it brings about far less total happiness. The case of an overloaded and sinking lifeboat also treats everyone the same way, but it saves no one!

Differently, the maximal production of good might also be achieved by awarding all the good to one person and none to anyone else. Presidential elections, state lotteries, and the Academy Awards illustrate situations where we might like to divide the "winnings" a little more fairly among the contenders, but can't without significantly lowering the total perceived value of the award. The converse is also true: A perfectly fair distribution is an equal distribution, but people tend to underestimate the value of common or shared goods. The lopsided preponderance of private goods and services over public goods and services in the United States illustrates the tendency to devalue societal goods and to overvalue those that mark individuality. Therefore, production of the most good does not necessarily mean that it will be distributed equitably.

A second well-known shortcoming of utilitarian analysis is its *preference for quantifiable criteria* over nonquantifiable but equally important variables. When businesses select new employees, for example, they are sometimes impressed more by quantifiable traits, such as typing speed, college grades, or size of the budget managed in the previous job, than by equally important but unmeasurable characteristics, such as interpersonal skills or loyalty. The obvious result is decisions based not on the best reasons, but on reasons that are compatible with the method. One writer, Abraham Kaplan, metaphorically described the utilitarian model of decision making as a "drunkard's search," in which a drunkard, who lost his keys some distance away, is looking for them under a lamppost. When asked why he is looking there, he replies, "Because that's where the light is."[5] So, one might argue that utilitarianism displays a quantitative bias that compels human beings to look at a problem in a particular way, to the exclusion of other possibly attractive options. Ida Hoos deftly portrayed the quantitative bias of utilitarian analysis when she said, "When the only tool you have is a hammer, everything else looks like nails."[6]

The preceding criticisms of utilitarian thinking are widely recognized, standard objections. A third and final criticism, however, is rarely recognized — perhaps because it relates exclusively to business practice, in particular, advertising. We will call it *preference manipulation*. If the best alternative is the one that is most generally satisfying, then one way of increasing satisfaction is to match available alternatives to existing preferences. But another way is to manipulate preferences in order to create increased satisfaction without changing the alternatives. That is, if personal preferences can be augmented or strengthened, greater satisfaction will be achieved in satisfying those preferences without changing the means by which they are satisfied.

So, utilitarian theory allows for, and even promotes, preference manipulation. This can be achieved through skillful advertising and campaigning. Fanning the fires of passion, promoting envy, and instilling fears that can be calmed through guided acquisitions in the marketplace are standard strategies of preference manipulation in advertising. (Hence, the saying, "You can sometimes sell what you can't give away.") Consequently, gluttony is promoted over a life of moderation and self-restraint on the grounds that greater total satisfactions are realized in the course of maximizing utility. Furthermore, whether one's needs are now few because they have been fully satisfied or because they were moderate to begin with is irrelevant for future utilitarian judgments; satiation and austerity are sometimes equivalent beginning points in making minimal demands upon future distributions of goods.

So, *utilitarianism* is the name given to one way of making decisions on ethical matters. It has been very influential in policy making worldwide and has generally promoted reasonability in areas where thought had been skewed through the force of custom, politics, or ideology. Despite its contribution to better thinking, however, it displays inherent shortcomings that convince us that we must remain responsible for our decisions regardless of what a method of thought recommends. But where those shortcomings begin to restrain confidence in our decisions, we are not without alternative guidelines for carrying on our ethical deliberations. The second approach to ethics, ethical formalism, is available to us, and it displays complementary strengths and weaknesses.

Formalism: Looking for Rules

In the case at the beginning of this chapter, suppose that the motive of the corporation's decision makers was truly sinister. That is, they were interested in personal success, which is measured in part by corporate success; they care little about the community or long-term health and safety; and they have no sympathy for those whose jobs might be lost. But suppose also that when they proceed with the secret dumping of toxic wastes, no environmental damage ever occurs. According to utilitarian calculations, this act may indeed have produced the greatest good for the greatest number, since it saved jobs, raised corporate profits, and in fact resulted in no degradation to the environment. That is, when the total consequences are summed, the original fears prove to be unfounded, and the benefits far outweigh the losses. Must we then conclude that this corporation was accidentally right in breaking the law and that evil motives generated good results?

For utilitarians, that may indeed be the proper conclusion. Since the worth of an act is determined simply by assessing its actual contribution to the general welfare, motives become less relevant. To illustrate this feature further, suppose that the corporate officers have only the best of motives: obey the law, preserve jobs, think of the long-term welfare of the community, and so on. Nevertheless, suppose also that in doing their best to act on these motives, everything goes wrong: Corporate profits fall in the face of competition, jobs are lost, the economy of the community suffers, the corporation is falsely accused of abandoning the town's interests, and so on. According to this scenario, the converse occurs: The best motives result in unforeseen disaster for all. The possibility that good motives go unrewarded is an actual experience for some people and an ethical issue for us all. So, how does one judge the moral worth of an act—by its consequences or by the motives of the agent?

Immanuel Kant

If utilitarianism measures the worth of an act by its consequences, ethical formalism assesses morality on the basis of personal motives. The major proponent of this view is Immanuel Kant.

If Jeremy Bentham's life was dramatic, or at least different, Kant's was not. Frederick Copleston provides this picture of the very ordinary life of a most important philosopher:

> We do not need to spend much time in recounting the facts of Kant's life. For it was singularly uneventful and devoid of dramatic incident. True, any philosopher's life is devoted primarily to reflection, not to external activity on the stage of public life. He is not a commander in the field or an Arctic explorer. And unless he is forced to drink poison like Socrates or is burned at the stake like Giordano Bruno, his life naturally tends to be undramatic. But Kant was not even a travelled man of the world like Leibniz. For he spent all his life in East Prussia. Nor did he occupy the position of a philosophical dictator in the university of a capital city, as Hegel did later at Berlin. He was simply an excellent professor in the not very distinguished university of a provincial town. Nor was his character such as to provide a happy hunting-ground for psychological analysts, as with Kierkegaard and Nietzsche. In his later years he was noted for his methodical regularity of life and for his punctuality; but it would hardly occur to anyone to think of him as an abnormal personality. But perhaps one can say that the contrast between his quiet and comparatively uneventful life and the greatness of his influence has itself a dramatic quality.[7]

Immanuel Kant was born at Konigsberg on April 22, 1724, the son of a saddler, and died in 1804. He studied at the local high school and later at the University of Konigsberg, where he met Martin Knutzen, a professor, who was probably the main influence on Kant. Fifty-seven years old when he published his first famous work, *The Critique of Pure Reason*, Kant defied the stereotype that innovation comes to the young and did all his major philosophical work in the last 23 years of his life.

The undramatic quality of Kant's daily life is well illustrated by his daily work routine, which has become famous:

> Rising shortly before five in the morning, he spent the hour from five to six drinking tea, smoking a pipe, and thinking over his day's work. From six to seven he prepared his lecture, which began at seven or eight, according to the time of year, and lasted until nine or ten. He then devoted himself to writing until the midday meal, at which he always had company and which was prolonged for several hours, as Kant enjoyed conversation. Afterwards he took a daily walk of an hour or so, and the evening was given to reading and reflection. He retired to bed at ten o'clock.[8]

But if his daily routine was ordinary, his contribution to ethical theory was not. Although not so well known to the general public as perhaps Plato or Aristotle, Kant is nevertheless widely regarded among professional philosophers as the greatest thinker of modern times. His most important works in ethics consist of *The Critique of Practical Reason* (1788) and *Foundations for a Metaphysic of Morals* (1785).

Pure Reason

The problem with a utilitarian outlook, as Kant sees it, is its failure to regard human behavior as intrinsically valuable. That is, the utilitarian is continually deciding what to do based not on the value of the action itself but on its consequences, which in turn are assessed in terms of their ability to satisfy human preferences. Consequently, nothing acquires moral stature in and of itself, but only in instrumental terms as a means to the satisfaction of some end. For a utilitarian, for example, telling the truth is moral because it gets good results, not because telling the truth per se is right.

Kant argues, therefore, that all utilitarian decisions are conditional; that is, the judgment of right and wrong ultimately depends on what human beings want. And although utilitarians might not agree that there is any criterion for the moral worth of actions beyond their contribution to the fulfillment of human purposes, Kant asserts that true moral judgments are independent of what any particular individual or group thinks. A statement like "Lying is wrong" may be morally correct whether we like it or not, even if no person alive tells the truth. As Bertrand Russell once said, "I find it quite intolerable to suppose that when I say 'Cruelty is bad' I am merely saying that I dislike cruelty." Similarly, Kant's goal is to account for how we might be able to know that some moral judgments are true regardless of anyone's personal opinions.

To do this, Kant appeals to the idea of *pure reason*, that is, to the possibility of discovering and knowing moral laws or principles without necessarily liking them or experiencing them, but just by recognizing their authenticity. The big question, of course, is, how do we recognize moral principles? (It's a big question because the answer implies the existence of absolute ethical principles that do not vary from person to person or from culture to culture.) Do they look different? Do they feel different? Do immoral principles, like human sacrifice or cannibalism, send chills down the spine? Perhaps there are no such things as absolute moral principles, and perhaps pure reason is only a ghostly idea.

Kant's answer is that human beings do have the capacity to recognize right from wrong and to agree on those judgments. He calls the faculty *pure reason*, indicating, however, that it is a fragile ability, the use of which greatly depends on the willingness of persons to trust in its promises. Pure reason is equivalent to pure motives, and the latter can easily be overwhelmed by an individual's personal preferences and private motives. When that happens, our ability to reason purely becomes contaminated with a variety of personal compulsions. One might not think clearly in an ethical situation because of a major mental or physical problem; or one might act improperly when one is merely hungry, selfish, afraid, or in love. Either way, for reasons large or small, people can fail to recognize or to do what ought to be done when circumstance or personal inclination presses upon their will.

But what Kant is interested in is the nature of ethical thinking apart from circumstance or personal feeling, that is, pure reason. If we were perfectly impartial and had no personal interest in the resolution of an issue, and if nothing were compelling us to decide in a particular way, how could we make the right decision? If our motives were pure and we were perfectly free to decide an issue, how would we go about doing it?

Universalizability

One characteristic of laws is that they apply to all equally. So, if there are moral laws, they must also apply to all. Kant asks us to consider, therefore, whether any given principle in question might reasonably be thought to apply universally. If it meets this requirement, it could be considered a moral law. For example, Kant illustrates this requirement as it applies to a person about to break a promise. It is not possible, he says, that promise breaking can be regarded as a universal law because if no one ever kept promises, no one would ever expect promises to be made and kept; therefore, no promise could be made and then broken. That is, the act of promise breaking depends upon the fact that people generally keep their promises. Promise breaking, therefore, is not possible as a universal law. Promise keeping, on the other hand, is universalizable; therefore, only the keeping of promises can be regarded as a moral law.

Reflecting upon the toxic waste case, we see that secretly using an unapproved dump site cannot be universalized. Even if there were no law regarding the disposal of toxic waste products and people could dump them anywhere they wished, the practice would run afoul of other universalizable principles, such as "Avoid harming others" and perhaps "Clean up your own messes." That is, the universalizability of a principle implies its consistency with all other moral principles; the complete collection of moral laws must "fit" each other without clashing. And the secret disposal of toxic wastes, when thought of as a general law, conflicts with other laws in the set; therefore, it is not accepted as a guide for moral behavior.

So, according to the formalistic criterion in ethics, an action must be lawful if it is to be recognized as a genuine ethical principle. That means that it must be consistent with itself, as well as with other principles in the set. In general, then, we might say that there is one overriding moral principle that serves as the foundation upon which all others rest. Kant calls it the *categorical imperative*, and one formulation is this: "So act that the maxim of your will could always hold at the same time as a principle establishing universal law."[9] This is a categorical imperative because it serves as an absolute guide for our behavior and is true regardless of what any person thinks or feels. Although Kant is not completely clear in explaining his categorical imperative, the following examples may be helpful.

Examples

Let's use the two examples that we used earlier to illustrate utilitarian thinking: pornography and legalization of gambling.

Regarding pornography, the formalist asks whether marketing the depiction of erotic behavior that is designed to cause sexual arousal can be universally allowed. There doesn't seem to be anything internally problematic about pornography; the problem lies in its relation to other principles, such as respect for others. Generally speaking, pornography abstracts the most essential features of human sexual relations, namely, respect, concern for privacy, and love, and displays love between individuals as mere cooperation in self-gratification. If this line of thought is correct, pornography is immoral from a formalistic perspective because it is inherently deceptive and untrue to other moral principles: It portrays human sexuality as something less than the full expression of some of the finest human feelings, and it publicizes a private act. (Note that this is very different reasoning from the utilitarian concern that pornography encourages forms of socially harmful behavior.)

The formalist analysis of gambling proceeds along similar lines. Like pornography, gambling violates some respected principles of behavior. It uncouples reward from merit and attributes wealth to mere chance. It distributes wealth in unequal ways for no apparent reason. Defending gambling by asserting its entertainment function fails to recognize its true appeal—getting something for nothing. What does such entertainment consist of if not the momentary possibility of gaining undeserved, accidental wealth? Gambling, therefore, is inherently subversive: The wish for instant success—even if only short-lived—contradicts trusted human experience regarding the attachment of growth and value to effort and work. This is illustrated in the life of the addicted gambler who is convinced beyond reason that luck will change and success is just around the corner. (Again, note how different this kind of thinking is from the utilitarian form of analysis, which weighs the positive and negative consequences of gambling in judging its worth.)

Strengths and Weaknesses

Perhaps the greatest strength of formalistic analysis in ethics is its collective logic. That is, the formalistic approach to ethics produces a *system* of principles or rules that "map out" acceptable behaviors and warn of questionable acts, much the way signs along a highway establish traffic rules and identify changes, dangers, or opportunities in advance. Even a single principle applies to more than the case at hand; it applies to all relevantly similar cases. If one employee is disciplined for chronic tardiness, every other employee with this problem should also be disciplined. The formalistic advantage lies in not having to decide every time whether discipline is the appropriate managerial response to habitual tardiness. To the formalist, good moral rules are more than rules of thumb; that is, they do more than suggest a good way to proceed based on recent experience. Moral rules *define* and *require*. In the game of baseball, for example, a rule of thumb might be "Don't try to hit a home run when all you need is a single." But a rule like "A batted ball that hits the chalk line is fair" is more than just a rule of thumb; it prescribes how the game must be played.[10]

So, like the rules of a game, the moral rules sought by formalistic reasoning provide direction and stability, boundaries and opportunities. They do not change from situation to situation. Instead, the collective logic supplied by a system of rules, like the Bill of Rights, connects our actions to a pattern of right and wrong behavior that serves as a standard meant to be emulated by all.

In building a system of rules, if formalistic reasoning works well, what is achieved is a collection of consistent, clear, and simple rules that are sufficient to resolve most disputes. Unfortunately, things do not often work out so well for formalistic systems. They have a tendency to become large and complex. This tendency toward *complexity* is the first major weakness of formalistic reasoning. It may be illustrated by the tax laws of the United States, where possibly hundreds of special rules are needed to specify what counts as an itemized deduction. Even such simple moral rules as "Do not tell a lie" and "Never kill another" are ambiguous and need further refinement. In business, large bureaucracies often develop very complex systems of rules that stereotypically illustrate the fate of many formal systems. This is to be expected for large organizations rather than small ones because in small organizations the kind of coordination provided by systems of rules is less urgent. Indeed, the difference between a professional bureaucracy and an entrepreneurial firm is reflected in a significant way in the differing dominant modes of decision making characteristic of each type.

A second weakness in formalistic reasoning is closely associated with the tendency toward large size and complexity; this is the tendency toward *dogmatism*. If anything is true of the stereotypic bureaucracy, it is its impenetrability and immovability. Likewise, if one places too much trust in a particular formulation of a rule, or if one is too tired or stressed to attend to the particular needs of a new situation, the easy way out is to hide behind the rule and simply enforce it. Absolute rules regarding right and wrong are an ideal or goal of formalistic thinking rather than an accomplishment. The test of universalizability is seldom completed because human beings are generally not capable of considering matters on a universal scale for any particular decision. Unanticipated possibilities always seem to arise, calling into question principles previously thought unassailable. So, one must constantly be alert for the exceptional case in order to escape the trap of excessive rigidity in the management of rules.

Organizational dogmatism is typical of large bureaucracies. It consists of large-scale formalization of organizational processes: There is a rule for everything. The rules then stifle individual discretion and creativity and promote the idea that satisfaction of the rules alone is sufficient for organizational success.

A third and final criticism of formalistic analysis in ethical decision making is its *tendency to treat all alike* and to ignore valuable idiosyncratic differences among individuals. Pincoffs's criticisms of ethical theory are relevant here (see Chapter Two). In trying to design general rules, we tend to abstract out idiosyncratic details of individuals' personalities, for example, that might be highly relevant in a particular situation. But individual personalities and style are important in ethics, and it is difficult to develop ethical rules that take into consideration such differences. Ethically speaking, for example, a confident and loud but affable manager might handle a confrontation with an employee in a way that differs considerably from that of a manager whose style is more calm and passive. The same thing may be accomplished in both cases, but the manner of achieving that result could hardly be the object of a single ethical principle.

We are left with a somewhat uncomfortable conclusion at the end of our review of decision making in ethics: We want one decision procedure or criterion for deciding what is right, but what we get is two! Intuitively, we feel that this is unacceptable because there is no obvious guarantee that the two procedures will always (or ever) agree. Furthermore, ethics seems to be one thing, not two—just as chemistry is one thing and music is one thing. Shouldn't ethics also consist of a single approach or method?

Many philosophers have argued the superiority of one view over the other; others have attempted to demonstrate the reduction of one view to the other. This book argues, to the contrary, that utilitarian and formalistic demands in ethics are equally valid. Each displays certain flaws, as we have seen, but neither method is avoidable. The next chapter takes up this issue in more detail and begins to show how utilitarian and formalistic reasoning provide complementary functions in ethics.

Summary of Key Concepts

1. Ethical theory basically consists of two approaches to decision making: utilitarianism and formalism.

2. Utilitarianism was first formulated by Jeremy Bentham. It rests upon three main assumptions:
   a. Decisions should achieve the greatest good for the greatest number.
   b. Goodness is defined in terms of pain and pleasure.
   c. Pains and pleasures are quantifiable and comparable phenomena.

3. Cost-benefit analysis is almost identical in structure to utilitarian analysis.

4. The strengths of utilitarian thinking include:
   a. Its liberality — All persons' preferences are equally important.
   b. Its ability to describe much of what we do when we make decisions.

5. The weaknesses of utilitarianism include:
   a. The problem of justice — Achieving the greatest good for the greatest number does not necessarily mean that *everyone* is treated well; the best *overall* results are compatible with the worst possible results for some *individual*.
   b. The bias in favor of quantifiable criteria — Some factors are harder to measure and compare than others.
   c. The encouraging of preference manipulation — The greatest good for the greatest number can be achieved by strengthening needs and wants; that is, through successful advertising, we can be persuaded to think that some alternative (or product) is more satisfying than we may have originally thought.

6. Immanuel Kant is the founder of ethical formalism. He was bothered by the utilitarian proposal that what is right may depend only on what people want. Instead, he believed that people are able to make judgments independent of their own wants and desires. He called this ability *pure reason* and described the process as searching for *universal moral principles*.

7. The strengths of formalism include:
    a. A system of coherent, stable, shared understanding
    b. A description of much of what we do, especially in bureaucracies
8. Its weaknesses include:
    a. The tendency toward complexity
    b. The tendency toward dogmatism
    c. The tendency to ignore important individual differences
9. Although utilitarianism and formalism have serious problems, these forms of ethical thinking are securely established in managerial decision making.

Questions and Exercises

1. A good piece of ethical advice often heard is something like this: "When you are having trouble deciding whether a given action is ethical, think of the three people you most respect (a parent, teacher, close friend, etc.) and try to imagine how they might feel about what you are considering." Is this recommendation utilitarian or formalist? Explain.

2. Regardless of whether one is mailing a letter across town or across the country, the postage is the same. Comment on this public policy from a utilitarian perspective and from a formalistic perspective.

3. A *tontine* is an agreement among two or more persons that resembles life insurance and was common in the United States prior to about 1850. It consists of a group of persons who contribute equal sums of money to a fund, with the fund being distributed among the survivors at the end of an agreed-upon period or, upon the death of all but one of the participants, to the lone survivor. Evaluate this practice from a utilitarian perspective and from a formalistic perspective.

4. Fairness can mean different things to different people. Little League baseball coaches, for example, often face the dilemma of deciding whether to play everyone or to play to win. Which choice would utilitarian analysis make? Which one would formalistic analysis make? Is it possible that utilitarian and formalistic analyses disagree on some issues? How about this one?

5. One of the most interesting characteristics of utilitarian analysis is that the rightness of a decision is judged by its actual results and not by the quality of the decision at the time it was made. Consider, for example, the situation of the National Aeronautics and Space Administration (NASA) officials just prior to the 1987 launch of the space shuttle *Challenger*. NASA was already far behind schedule and was facing funding cuts from Congress. The newspapers were fanning the fires of expectation. Everyone

wanted to see a launch. Every previous launch had been successful, and there were only engineering reports that stated that the O-ring seals might not perform properly under freezing conditions.

a. How do you think the general public would have regarded a NASA decision not to launch if in fact they had not launched?

b. Do you think that the Morton-Thiocol engineers suddenly felt immoral when they saw the *Challenger* explode?

c. Even if the problems *could not possibly* have been foreseen, can a utilitarian justify a decision to launch, given the disastrous results that followed?

6. Some university student newspapers carry ads from small companies that sell copies of research papers to students. Some of these companies advertise more than 16,000 titles and sell them for about $5 per page.

a. Is there anything unethical about selling copies of research papers?

b. Is a newspaper unethical when running ads for such services?

c. Can the practice of running such ads be defended by appealing to the principle of liberality, namely, that "we allow our readers to make up their own minds regarding the ads"?

d. Could a policy be designed that would prohibit research paper ads without ruling on any other form of advertising (such as alcohol ads)?

7. Consider the following case: The committee of a Boy Scouts of America camporee (a large weekend campout for 300 boy scouts) has met one week before the camporee to review plans and to take care of last-minute details. The committee has a small fund of $1,000 in donations from sponsoring churches and other organizations to pay for camp shirts, special patches, food for the staff, and a variety of other camporee expenses. The clerk, one of only two persons whose signatures are legally approved to sign checks drawing upon the fund, has informed the committee that he will be out of town the entire weekend

of the camporee. The second person whose signature is approved is difficult to find, is not present at the committee meeting, and is unlikely to spend much time at the camporee. A member of the committee who needs to pick up some of the awards and ribbons to be handed out at the conclusion of the camporee requests a blank check to be signed now by the clerk and filled out later in the week when the awards are picked up from a local engraving firm.

a. What would a utilitarian do? A formalist?
b. What is the right thing to do? Is there any way to balance the two views?

C H A P T E R

4

A Janus-Headed View of Ethical Theory

The aim of this chapter is to call attention to the need for a clearer understanding of the contribution of ethical theory to management ethics and to propose a model of ethical theory that will begin to facilitate that understanding and provide a foundation on which considerable detail can be added in subsequent chapters. The most important point is that whereas the relation between formalist and utilitarian ethics has traditionally been antagonistic, the schema developed here asserts their *complementarity*. The relation of formalism and utilitarianism is not a zero-sum relation; it is more like a division of labor. In the following section, the theoretical foundations of this schema are presented.

A Janus-Headed View of
Ethical Processes in Society

Whether ethical theory is considered an acquisition of timeless principles, an unchanging infallible method, or something else, its application to business or management results in a *process*. That is, the corporation's responsibility to the social milieu that sustains it represents a continuous adjustment of interests. This does not mean that the process is an unanchored, undirected Hobbesian "war of all against all." On the contrary, the relationships to be discussed assume that societal processes of ethical adjustment have both anchor and destination; but the anchor is more like a constantly moving sea anchor, and the destination is more of a navigational aid than an ending of the journey. More specifically, rather than portraying utilitarian and formalist ethics in the traditional philosophical way as antagonists, the view to be developed asserts their compatibility and complementarity.

The Roman god Janus, the god of gates and entryways, is depicted as having two faces—one facing forward and the other backward. Temporally speaking and applied to ethics, this view portrays the social process of resolving ethical issues as simultaneously looking to the past as well as to the future. And by both intuitive appeal and argumentative assertion, this view classifies utilitarians as the forward-looking component and formalists as oriented primarily to the past. That is, formalists tend to be interested in the past as it appears in language, tradition, and precedent, while utilitarians approach ethical issues by looking to the future for anticipated results, opportunities, and innovation. In this way, current social practices form a nexus that links (if uncomfortably) tradition and change, restraint and opportunity, language and invention.

With this new Janus-headed analogy in mind, then, we can more fully describe the predicament of business leaders who find themselves caught on the horns of a dilemma between organizational rationality and public perception. At any given moment, those who are confronted with the task of ethical decisions are doing two things:

1. They are looking to the cultural heritage established by law, language, and tradition and assessing the relevance and adequacy of the store of knowledge to the issue at hand.

2. They are simply seeking to discover a solution that will bring about the best possible results according to some idea of what it means to be fully human. (Since the latter requirement is a notoriously difficult one, utilitarians usually liberalize it by surveying the personal preferences of all interested or affected persons, rather

than explicate and defend some concept of essentially human goals or ends.)

In other words, the arena in which business-society issues are discussed has *two simultaneous interests*. One involves the need to reconcile new practices with accumulated wisdom being "pulled along behind" as various forms of "cultural baggage" that serve to charter current behavior and thought. The trailing "net of custom" provides a contextual form of objectivity, thereby achieving coherence and consistency. This form of ethical objectivity implies a continual adjustment of the net: adding, deleting, modifying, and so on. Any given principle acquires contextual objectivity to the degree to which its position in the net is secure and comfortable (discussed in detail in Chapter Six).

How Formalism Is Retrospective

The connection between formalism and the restrospective element in this model can be made more carefully. As we learned in Chapter Three, Kant's categorical imperative, often characterized as the best example of a formalistic method, requires universalizability. That is, one's actions are morally prescribed only in the case where all other persons in similar circumstances could be required to act the same way. What this, in turn, necessitates is some principle or maxim that adequately captures the ethical essence of the situation. Such a procedure is needed in order to be able to identify other relevantly similar situations to which the principle also would apply. The various ethical codes designed by professions and corporations are good examples of collections of these kinds of principles. Alternatively, if ethical principles were not designed to subsume a wide range of actions under a simple rule, universalizing would become so situation specific and so tied to the idiosyncratic features of each case that any principle relating to a particular case would suffer immediate obsolescence. (For example, the principle "Thou shalt not lie" would reduce to "Thou shalt not lie *this time*" for some perhaps subtle reasons.) Indeed, formalists continually defend themselves against the challenge of exceptions to every rule. Thus, if the

63

universalizability requirement is illusory, then ethics explodes into countless fragments of unshared intuitions regarding isolated personal experiences. Each person would have his or her own idea about ethics. Alternatively, the force of Kant's universalizability requirement is to avoid this ethically unacceptable consequence by demanding a set of ethical principles that will promote consistency and understanding from case to case.

For these reasons, most formalistic positions in the business-society area look more like *conceptual* arguments, since the formalists inquire into the features of a given case that enable them to generalize their findings to similar cases. Consequently, the refinement of principles through the use of analogies and counterexamples is a good sign that formalists are at work on the net of custom.

How Utilitarianism Is Prospective

The second, forward-looking activity of ethics, here called *utilitarianism*, is often referred to as being *teleological, consequentialist,* or *end-result ethics*. It virtually ignores the cultural heritage in order to focus on concrete cases and their resolution. According to utilitarianism, each new issue requires only that the best possible results be sought, regardless of what has been done in the past. Innovation, invention, and optimal results are important here. "We have *this* problem *here*, and we have it *now*; what do we *do* next?" This second side of social ethical processes reminds us that although ethics seeks consistency and coherence, it may sacrifice them in order to pursue the best results. Thus, past practices and understandings do not preclude freely choosing new practices, improving techniques, or changing beliefs and preferences.

The temporal contrast of formalist and utilitarian approaches to ethics implies a handful of related contrasts and does not exhaust the range of characterizations of the two positions. For example, formalists tend to be more abstract and utilitarians more concrete because of the nature of each approach: Formalists seek general principles, which forces them to abstract from ethical situations only the relevant features for use in other similar cases, while utilitarians can afford to give greater attention to all details of a case, especially as they influence results. So, we might also say that formalists seek ethical understanding, while utilitarians seek results. This can be illustrated in a practical context by the way some people might shop for binoculars: Interested in results, the utilitarian simply compares the optical quality and maintenance record of each and buys the least expensive binoculars of the desired quality. The formalist, by contrast, may buy the same binoculars but does so for different reasons. *That* a pair of binoculars is good is not enough; one must also know *why* it is good, and that involves knowing something about optical design and the generalizable engineering features that account for quality from type to type.

Other psychological contrasts between the two views can be listed briefly:

Utilitarianism	*Formalism*
novelty, progress, change	stability, pattern
case-by-case results	consistency
democratic	authoritarian
fluid	rigid
accuracy	clarity
compromise	agreement
specificity	simplicity
rules of thumb	principles

Much of the argumentative support for each of these pairs of contrasts is supplied in subsequent chapters, but the reader may consider them now in order to get a quick picture of the two positions. (Given the psychological nature of many of these contrasts, it is natural to suppose that some persons, because of their own psychological makeup, may be inclined to use one manner of ethical thinking or the other. Therefore, you may wish to take the diagnostic test in the Appendix to obtain a quick reading of your own propensities toward formalism or utilitarianism in your approach to ethical issues.)

Plausibility of a theory is provided by more than arguments. A new idea that provides an immediate practical payoff will be taken seriously enough, and indeed, much of the rest of this chapter seeks to provide precisely that form of justification for this new approach to ethical theory.

Application to Current Business-Society Issues

If the process view of ethics described earlier, which I refer to as a *Janus-headed analogy*, is to be useful, we should expect to construct a set of Janus-headed issues that illustrate features of the view. That is, some problems should reflect this tension between tradition and freedom, resulting in two distinct thrusts or "issue pairs" on some topics.

The Dual Nature of Some Problems

The general issue of coporate trade secrets illustrates how one issue really becomes two. The formalist side of the problem is essentially an adjustment of the rights of corporate owners to retain a competitive advantage with the rights of individual employees to market their skills.[1] How does one draw the line between marketable skills incidentally acquired on the job and knowledge or techniques that are the property of the corporation? This is the conceptual issue faced by the formalists. The utilitarians, by contrast, simply want to devise some arrangement that will reduce the antagonism between the actors and be acceptable to both parties. Some suggestions, for example, might include pensions or consulting contracts that distribute money to former employees on the condition that they do not work for a competitor for specified number of years.[2] The important point here, however, is that the problem of the disclosure of corporate trade secrets has a dual identity. There are really *two issues* corresponding to the natural tension between (1) the need for a principle to serve as a criterion for consistency and (2) the concrete need to resolve a present conflict in the best possible manner. The issues are:

1. How to weigh the property rights of the firm against the personal rights of the employees.
2. How to achieve a workable solution short of issuing a legal pronouncement.

In like manner, a number of business-society issues are manifested as issues pairs:

1. *Whistleblowing*

   a. The formalist needs a way to think, a standard for alleviating the conflict between organizational loyalty and personal conscience.[3] What is a rule by which an employee will know that one's obligation of loyalty to the organization is overridden by one's obligation as a citizen to make an urgent matter public?

   b. The utilitarian focuses on the means to reduce the structural impediments to information flow in organizations.[4] Why are people with problems often ignored in organizations, and what can be done about it?

2. *Corporate Bribery Overseas*

   a. Formalists need clear guidelines, such as the distinction between bribery and "grease payments." They discuss the propriety of exporting values, as well as problems of cultural relativism.[5] Whose rule should one operate by—those of one's own country or those of the host country? Should one always "do in Rome as the Romans do"?

   b. Utilitarians focus on the workability of various proposed solutions, such as the Foreign Corrupt Practices Act.[6] Does requiring American corporations not to pay bribes (like everyone else) put them at a disadvantage? How can we get other countries to cooperate in conforming to some consistent standards of behavior?

3. *Ecology and Pollution Control*

   a. Formalists tend to focus on the nature of the relation between human beings and their environment: whether forms of nonhuman life have rights, and so on.[7] They also examine the rights of persons to health and safety.[8] Pollution control is a matter of identifying correct standards and enforcing those standards through a system of penalties and other means.

      b. The utilitarian is typically interested in assessing the consequences of various practices, such as toxic waste dumping and nuclear power, and the relative merits of proposed solutions. Pollution control could be achieved through a more marketlike system of fees and pollution credits, as opposed to establishing standards for toxicity.

  4. *Software Piracy*

      a. The issue for the formalist is whether ownership rights should be recognized, making illegal free copying, or whether such products are not unique creations and should be treated with minimal market protection, like any other product. Maybe there is nothing seriously wrong with pirating software.

      b. From the utilitarian perspective, the issue is more practical: how to avoid the administratively costly problem of fighting a black market in software and still provide incentives and remuneration for the creators of software. If software piracy were declared legal, how much damage would be done to software production? How can software be constructed to make piracy increasingly difficult or expensive?

So, as implied by the proposed model, at least some business-society questions are in reality issue pairs that reflect the underlying dual nature of ethical processes in society.

Utilitarian Issues

Not all business-society issues reflect formalist and utilitarian interests equally. Contrary to the traditional view of ethical theory, which asserts the equal (if competitive) application of formalist and utilitarian methods to all problems, this new view allows for the existence of issues in which ethical attention seems to shift significantly toward either formalist or utilitarian concerns. According to the Janus-headed analogy, for example, if the technology of a traditional business practice were improved, resulting in dramatically changed consequences, the utilitarians would be quick to examine the practice (because of their interest in securing better results), while the formalists might lag behind (because the essential nature of the practice had not changed).

Consider, for example, the morality of genetic engineering in high-tech firms. The discussions in the literature focus predominantly on the utilitarian interest in weighing potential hazards against the promises of success in achieving a variety of technological breakthroughs.[9] How hazardous to human welfare is the attempt to create new life forms, like altered bacteria or modified viruses? Is the potential benefit to humankind greater than the cost and the risk of accident or unforeseen disasters? And so on.

The formalistic interests in this new practice are weak, and they tend to be religious: What right do humans have to tamper with God's creations? For business administrators and teachers, however, this seems to be far less signficant than the utilitarian question.

The cause of the skewed attention paid to this issue can be explained by appeal to the Janus-headed analogy in that despite its exotic, high-tech image, genetic experimentation with viruses and bacteria is a traditional activity with unexplored consequences. It is not significantly different in form from producing new strains of roses, orchids, corn, or fruitflies— standard practices in Western business activity. Seen in this light, recombinant DNA experiments are the high-tech equivalent of making a better mousetrap. If this explanation is correct, genetic engineering attracts less formalistic analysis because it is not yet seen to be qualitatively different from accepted practices in business tradition, even though it may be extending the range of consequences beyond the usual.

Of course, this situation could change dramatically if the techniques develop to a point where the genetic engineering of human beings becomes achievable. That may mark a qualitative change that would require lengthy formalistic analysis to determine whether the net of tradition could be adjusted to allow for such practices.

Other business-society issues that appear to emphasize

utilitarian questions rather than formalistic ones are (1) nuclear power and (2) the production of nuclear arms. What makes both of these issues so utilitarian is the difficulty of assessing the probabilities attached to the worst-case scenario for each issue. Does the improbable but persistent threat of disaster outweigh the benefits of reduced energy costs or military deterrence?

Indeed, the potential for disaster in these cases is so striking that many thinkers have felt compelled to enlarge the discussion by invoking more formalistic considerations, such as (1) the changing attitudes toward civilian immunity during war, (2) the morality and logic of the intention to destroy, and (3) the morality of accepting potential devastation as a component of modern life.[10] Thus, these issues are not exclusively utilitarian, but they are dominantly utilitarian. And at least part of the explanation for the utilitarian focus in both cases, arguably, is that we are not doing anything qualitatively new in either case—just bigger, better, faster, and so on. We have been making both electricity and weapons for a long time.

Formalistic Issues

Even though issues such as those just discussed draw predominantly utilitarian attention, traditional practices may be questioned at any time. Societies are not immune to making big mistakes. Therefore, the possibility of formalist analyses that go beyond evaluation of the new practices to an evaluation of the tradition itself gives a reason to suppose that the comparative absence of any formalist discussion on issues such as those just discussed is due to the strength of the connection between the practice in question and the dominant ideology or world view. The formalist perspective is only latent; it is not nonexistent.

For example, until the early 1960s, the lack of civil rights for blacks in the United States was not perceived as a severe distortion of the social tradition. Only when the internal inconsistencies were repeatedly pointed out did society begin to realize that its net of custom was malformed and needed repair.

As a special case of civil rights, the issue of justice in employment practices seems to represent the alternative form of skewness in the Janus-headed model, where analytical attention appears to be predominantly formalistic. Throughout most discussions of employment discrimination, this issue seems to be a formalistic one: Should a business owner have a right to hire anyone he or she pleases, or must employment criteria be job related? Is mere equality of treatment adequate to compensate for accumulated injustices? What is meant by *discriminated minority*? Is discrimination a matter of doing justice to disadvantaged individuals or to a class of persons? And so on. (The issue can be regarded from the utilitarian perspective as the practical or political problem of satisfying the demands of certain groups, but the various proposed programs are usually evaluated in terms of their *fairness*, and not merely their results.)

Other standard issues that seem to generate formalistic rather than utilitarian concerns are the nature of the corporation and employee freedom of expression:

1. *The Nature of Corporations.* The issue is exclusively formalistic: Should corporations, not just individuals, be regarded as moral entities to be held accountable to society?[11] And if corporations are to be held responsible, what punishments are appropriate — imprisonment, death, or just penalties and fines?

2. *Employee Freedom of Expression.* Should employees be allowed to criticize the organization? Where does organizational loyalty end and individual freedom of expression begin? Here the formalist must balance rights against each other and provide principles for making judgments.

Again, an account of the marked shift toward formalist concerns while ignoring utilitarian views is supplied by the Janus-headed analogy. In each case, the consequences of a practice are less important than our *justification* of the practice. The need is to understand how the practice either is or is not consistent with other beliefs, ideas, and principles in the traditional scheme of things.

So, whether business-society topics seem balanced or

skewed in terms of the attention paid them by the two sides of the model presented here, ethical process in society might be viewed as a continual reconciliation of "the way things are done" with "a new way to do things." The Australian victory in the 1983 Americas Cup contest was an excellent example of the confrontation between traditional guidelines (contained in the rule book) and technological innovation (the winged keel).

Both formalism and utilitarianism may be taken to excess. On the one hand, failure to employ vision and imagination may lead to obsolescence or dogmatism. On the other hand, to ignore the stabilizing effect of tradition and to allow imagination to run too far ahead of rigor in the social process may lead to loss of coherence and clarity — something resembling societal insanity. The problem, as Bateson put it, is a matter of timing:

> How shall change in form be *safely* speeded up to avoid obsolescence? And how shall descriptions of change in functioning be summarized and coded, not too fast, into the corpus of form?[12]

Traditional views of the relation between utilitarian and formalist ethical theories have not anticipated such developments, and yet they are consistent with, if not implied by, the process model argued for here. If true, the new view points to the urgent need to establish the legitimate social responsibility of business in light of the realization that business itself, by promoting technological advance, is on the leading edge of society's ethical process.

Advantages of the Janus-Headed View

Contrary to traditional views of ethical theory, the model developed here emphasizes a cluster of distinguishing features that together manifest a temporal theme: Formalists are retrospective and utilitarians are prospective. Additionally, this theory asserts the complementary functions of utilitarian and formalistic interests, skirting the antagonisms that naturally arise when each view is regarded by its proponents as the exclusive decision procedure in ethical matters.

Basis in Observation

One of this view's chief virtues is its more direct connection to the modern world of business ethics. The Janus-headed view of ethical theory is, first, expository: It clarifies the most general patterns of ethical reasoning as they are actually found in discussions of business-society issues. The theory accounts for the observation that formalism and utilitarianism do not apply with equal analytic power to all issues or problems. Its explanation for this observation appeals simply to an interesting asymmetry in ethical theory: Formalists emphasize the acquisition of consistent patterns of action (remembering that inconsistency is a *prima facie* case against morality), whereas utilitarians are more inclined to search for improved conditions and performance. Consequently, as issues arise at the business-society interface, some will attract more attention from utilitarians, while others will require formalistic treatment.

By focusing on discussions of ethical issues as they are currently found in the business-society literature, this view seeks to achieve relevance first by providing a natural typology of issues in business ethics and second by accounting for the typology without appealing to esoteric moral notions or technical jargon.

Freedom from Technical Jargon

By adopting a temporal distinction rather than a traditional methodological one, the Janus-headed view avoids some of the technical twists and turns of any particular formalistic or utilitarian theory. There is less need to talk of universalizing, moral absolutism, and categorical imperatives, for example, which comprise much of Kant's brand of formalism (even though great insight can be gained by studying his ideas closely).

The language used to present and develop the Janus-headed analogy is comparatively unsophisticated. Its purpose is to describe and persuade rather than to define, distinguish, and dissect. Its reliance on philosophical tradition is minimal. (A more detailed analysis of formalism as a component of the Janus-headed analogy is presented in Chapter Six.)

Utilitarian Indeterminacy as an Asset

Finally, the Janus-headed theory helps us to regard the indeterminacy or openness of utilitarianism as an asset rather than a liability. Utilitarian techniques are notorious for their inability to achieve closure.[13] This lack of determinacy is illustrated by several well-known "open ends" concerning:

1. Whether the best alternative has been identified
2. Whether all relevant criteria have been identified
3. The relative importance of each criterion
4. The quantifiability of certain nonquantifiable criteria
5. The indifference of utility maximization techniques to alternative distributions of costs and benefits
6. The probabilistic nature of anticipated consequences

Instead of regarding indeterminacy as a liability, the model adopted in this chapter views it as an asset — an important opportunity to choose direction and to assert value. Indeed, the strength of utilitarian thinking lies in the open invitation to ignore the constraints of traditional thought and the inertia of traditional value and, instead, to consider imaginatively the worth of both new practices and new values. One purpose of Jeremy Bentham's original development of utilitarian ethics, for example, was to promote progressive legislation and social reform.

A full argument for the openness of utilitarian thought is presented in the next chapter. And surely this needs to be done, since several writers have argued to the contrary: that the tendency of utilitarian reasoning as traditionally practiced is conservative rather than innovative: that it defends the status quo, promotes the reigning ideology, and circumvents value-forming processes in society.[14] The Janus-headed analogy, however, asserts that these are not intrinsic features of utilitarian thinking and that a nontraditional orientation may avoid much of the determinacy referred to in these objections. Again, utilitarianism is highly indeterminate, and this is an asset in ethics that balances the more determinate and analytic aspects of formalism.

Although the new view developed here may not fully satisfy the need to secure relevance for the application of ethical theory to business-society issues, it at least posits a context within which ethical theory is more meaningfully related to such matters. Much work remains to be done in developing this Janus-headed view in succeeding chapters. For example, we need to study the patterns of conceptual thinking manifested in formalistic reasoning, and we need to be more specific about the practical uses of utilitarian analysis—especially for managers. Furthermore, we need to give closer consideration to how these two positions interact in business.

Summary of Key Concepts

1. Like the Roman god Janus, who could see forward and backward simultaneously, ethical decision making requires a constant view from both the utilitarian and formalist perspectives.

2. Formalism is retrospective because it seeks precedent and consistency with past behavior, regardless of future consequences.

3. Utilitarian thinking is prospective because obtaining good results requires the anticipation of likely consequences for each alternative under consideration. Tradition, experience, and previous solutions are unimportant except as historical suggestions that may or may not be relevant for solving current problems.

4. Some issues are dominantly utilitarian, others dominantly formalistic. That is, most ethical issues require either a utilitarian or a formalistic approach. Some ethical issues are legitimately Janus-headed, meaning that both utilitarian and formalistic approaches are relevant. In such cases, however, the issue itself splits into two related issues, each corresponding to the utilitarian or formalistic perspective.

Questions and Exercises

1. From your regular reading of newspapers, journals, or magazines, make a list of the ethical issues you encounter and then decide what kind of issue each is — utilitarian, formalistic, or Janus-headed. Explain.

2. Choose an essay on an ethical issue and identify all the utilitarian and formalistic statements or arguments in the margin.

3. Take the diagnostic test in the Appendix. Compare your score with that of others in the class or group. Would you expect the differences to account for later disagreements in the class or group when discussing complex issues?

4. What kind of person, utilitarian or formalist, do you think would best fit in the following occupations or positions and why? Accountant, lawyer, entrepreneur, salesperson, religious leader. Can you think of other occupations or social positions that seem to reflect either utilitarian or formalistic characteristics?

5. Think of a formalistic issue, such as deciding what is and is not a conflict of interest. Even though we seem to be trying to decide what should be done in the future, this is really an issue that involves retrospection. Explain.

6. "Politicians are utilitarians trying to masquerade as formalists." Evaluate this claim.

7. What kind of person makes the best administrator — a utilitarian or a formalist? Does your answer depend on the nature of the organization or task? Explain.

8. Some researchers have found a correlation between formalistic reasoning and increasing age. How might one account for this finding?

9. A special project: Review and evaluate the concept of property as it has legally developed over the decades through Supreme Court decisions. (Hint: This is a Janus-headed issue. In the earlier cases, such as *Home Building and Loan Association*, v. *Blaisdell*, the Court's resolution of the issue of property was utilitarian, always favoring re-

lationships that promised a general increase in wealth and prosperity, even when it violated traditional property rights. In more recent cases, however, the task of the Court has been formalistic. As new forms of wealth have appeared, such as social security benefits, government contracts, occupational licenses, business franchises, public service employment, and welfare payments, the Court has increasingly recognized the right of individuals to lay claim to them, as opposed to regarding them, for example, as government gratuities or charity. Such cases were formalistic in that the Court needed to decide whether these new forms of wealth were to be regarded as property or not.)

10. Managers often face the issue of promoting on the basis of seniority or performance. Which of these decisions is more firmly grounded in formalistic reasoning? Which in utilitarian reasoning?

11. Ski resorts often exaggerate skiing conditions in daily reports. They report more snow than is actually present, or they report the depth of snow at the summit, rather than at the base. Examine this practice from the standpoint of both utilitarian and formalistic ethics.

12. Should a corporation compensate its marketing employees through wages or through a commission on sales? Which perspective is formalistic? Which is utilitarian?

13. The issue of the merit of hostile takeovers is generally discussed from a utilitarian perspective, that is, in terms of its worth to the U.S. economy. Some authors argue that allowing hostile takeovers weeds out poorly managed firms and reallocates capital in promising directions. Others argue that the practice creates chaos in terms of the defenses companies often take to prevent themselves from being taken over. Still other authors argue that, like nations, companies have a right to defend themselves.
    a. What is the general utilitarian impact of such strategies as poison pills, golden parachutes, selective buybacks, and so on?
    b. Is the short-term utilitarian picture of hostile takeovers different from the long-term picture?

c. From the formalistic point of view, are companies more like nations, which have a right to defend themselves, or like sharks, which devour weaker elements in the ecosystem?

d. Is the issue of hostile takeovers, then, dominantly utilitarian, formalistic, or Janus-headed?

5

Managerial Utilitarianism — A Theory of Adequate Reason

The major goal of the previous chapter was to call attention to the enormous gulf that exists between theory and practice in standard academic discussions of business ethics and to introduce a perspective that begins to bridge that gulf. But the Janus-headed theory presented in Chapter Four is only a beginning; the distance separating theory and practice in business ethics is still considerable. This is illustrated in academics, by the inability of theorists to produce and develop a practical method in ethics, and in practice by the all too common newspaper headlines calling attention to breaches of ethics by both private and public sector executives.

There are two ways to reduce the separation of theory and practice. One is to bring practice closer to theory, and the other is to move theory closer to practice. The traditional approach in business ethics is the former: A stable body of ethical theory exists, and students and practitioners alike are urged to conform in their thinking to theoretical standards. Contrary to tradition, this chapter and the next take the latter approach. They do so by infusing theory with a heavy dose of practice.

More specifically, this chapter focuses on utilitarian ethics and explores a managerial theory of utilitarianism that draws

81

far closer to the real-world need of most managers to think carefully but quickly about frequent issues of utility.

The Classical Theory and Its Flaws

We begin by reviewing some of the standard features of the classical model of utilitarian ethics, as presented in earlier chapters.

Utilitarianism is commonly regarded in business ethics as a stepwise decision procedure that seeks to select from a set of alternatives the action that is most likely to yield the best overall results. The precise description of the steps varies somewhat from author to author, but three essential assumptions of traditional utilitarianism seem invariant:

1. **Maximization of Good.** We should always seek to produce the greatest possible good for as many persons as possible who may be affected by our actions or decisions. Jeremy Bentham referred to this as the *greatest happiness principle.*[1] It is closely related to such modern concerns as welfare economics and the business principle of optimal productivity through efficiency. According to this assumption, it would be ethically wrong to settle for anything but the optimal alternative; a merely satisfactory result is ethically inferior.

2. **Comprehensive Measurement and Comparison of Goods.** Utilitarian analysis requires the quantitative measurement of goods. Similar to modern cost-benefit analysis, utilitarianism from the beginning has been committed to systematic analysis and comparison of the range of consequences attached to any given act. The possibility that even the most subjective goods could be objified through systematic analysis has had great appeal to modern economists. (The degree to which this is possible is currently a matter of debate.)

3. *Value-Based Determinism.* Persons' values have *logical* priority in any form of utilitarian ethics because they are the starting point of moral assessment. But they are also thought to exist *temporally* prior, as givens that are consulted to select the optimal alternative. The greatest good is achieved by satisfying existing but unsatisfied preferences. This is a "democratic" approach to utilitarianism: Because agreement on what constitutes the good life is unsecured, the optimal alternative simply becomes that action that achieves the greatest overall satisfaction, regardless of the nature of the wants or needs. Thus, existing values or preferences (rather than ideal values) determine moral choice.

Conjoining these three assumptions, utilitarian analysis has taken a variety of closely related forms. Sometimes it is referred to as the *maximizing model* of moral choice. James March has asserted that utilitarianism is a "matter of faith in important segments of contemporary Western civilization" and has described its "major tenets" as follows:

> Human beings make choices. If done properly, choices are made by evaluating alternatives in terms of goals on the basis of information currently available. The alternative that is most attractive in terms of the goals is chosen. The process of making choices can be improved by using the technology of choice. Through the paraphernalia of modern techniques, we can improve the quality of the search for alternatives, the quality of information, and the quality of the analysis used to evaluate alternatives. Although actual choice may fall short of this ideal in various ways, it is an attractive model of how choices should be made by individuals, organizations, and social systems.[2]

Utilitarianism's influence is pervasive in policy-making circles in Western society, and it has inspired various systems of analysis. Although it is probably most closely related to cost-benefit analysis, it is the philosophical grandfather of several analytical techniques now referred to generally as *systems analysis*. Despite their widespread use, utilitarian procedures are not without their shortcomings, and many authors have duly noted them.[3] Defenders of the utilitarian faith generally reply that the defects refer to shortcomings in human knowledge and skill rather than in the theory itself. However, management research over the last three or four decades has raised further doubts concerning the theoretical soundness of classical utilitarianism.

Adequacy as a Descriptive Theory

Generally speaking, utilitarianism was never intended to provide a good description of how people actually go about making ethical decisions. Its best use is as a prescriptive theory of moral behavior. That is, it serves to clarify what people ought to do and how they ought to think, even though in fact it might not describe very well the mental processes persons use when they deliberate on ethical issues. Nevertheless, there is good reason to hope that an ethical theory does a good job of both prescribing and describing. The more a theory differs in form from normal decision-making processes, the less relevant it becomes. So long as a good prescriptive theory also provides a close description, prescriptions are accompanied by practical insights into the nature of the mental processes leading to those prescriptions. But if a theory differs strongly from actual decision-making processes, the theory can act only as an external check on the *ends* of human ethical deliberation; it remains mute regarding the *means* to improve that thinking.

Scholars in the field of management have studied decision-making processes for years and have concluded that the maximizing model infrequently describes what people do in making ethical decisions. In the 1950s, Herbert Simon published two papers that indicated that decision making in organizations seldom fulfills classical utilitarian requirements.[4] Instead of searching for the best alternatives, managers were often observed to select merely satisfactory alternatives. As a general label for such processes, Simon coined the term *satisficing*.

Following Simon's lead, later studies confirmed his observations and described managerial decision making as being *bounded*, *constrained*, or *limited*. Lindblom, for example, distinguished between traditional comprehensive analysis and an incremental approach he aptly called *muddling through*, which he argued was actually a better description of public policy-making processes.[5] Cyert and March challenged the assumption of profit maximization as a description for managerial behavior, suggesting instead that firms seek only satisfactory profits while pursuing other goals selected by management.[6] Soelberg found that decision-making processes seldom involve the comparative weighting of factors required by classical utilitarianism.[7] And several studies have found that people do not make choices based upon prior and independently existing goals or values; instead, values and choices are developed simultaneously through decision experiences.[8]

Consequently, during the last 30 years, management theorists have almost univocally rejected the classical utilitarian model as an adequate descriptive theory of human decision making. Of course, Jeremy Bentham never intended to describe how people think; he was interested in showing them how they ought to think. Nevertheless, a theory of moral decision making must have some relevance or connection to human decision-making processes, or else it will be too esoteric and will be ignored. And what the management theorists are saying is that classical utilitarianism does not adequately describe the processes of deliberation used by managers. Therefore, we need *both* in one: a theory that shows us how to think and what to do. A merely prescriptive theory of decision making is blind to normal deliberative processes, while an exclusively descriptive theory may be powerless to guide action. We need a decision procedure.

Adequacy as a Reliable Method

Going further, not only does the classical normative method often fail to describe human decision-making behavior, there is evidence that application of the method sometimes produces inferior results.

One series of criticisms comes from critics of general systems theory. As we saw in the preceding chapter, utilitarianism has a built-in bias toward quantifiable variables, often resulting in arbitrary results. Anthony Downs calls attention to the arbitrariness induced by the method as used in public policy analysis, and he describes the result as "horse and rabbit stew": Only the most tractable variables (the rabbit) are analyzed, while the incommensurable variables (the horse) are ignored. He concludes, "We are making a stew with a scientifically-prepared rabbit and a randomly-chosen horse. The quality of such a stew is bound to be rather indeterminate."[9] The lesson here is that utilitarian theory itself is biased in favor of those variables that are most amenable to quantitative comparison; a more rational theory would avoid such bias, or at least be biased for better reasons.[10]

A second set of criticisms comes from economics. Heiner has argued that, as a prescriptive model, utility maximization produces inferior results.[11] Giving dozens of examples, he shows how the maximization model introduces indeterminacy into behavior, rather than reducing it. He argues that often a stubborn commitment to a repertoire of familiar behaviors produces better results than frequent tentative adjustments involving unusual or uncommon behaviors. Similarly, Elster examines the rationality of commitment to a course of action despite new information contradicting the chosen course. Recalling the story of Ulysses, who bound himself to the mast of his ship with instructions to be ignored if he appeared to change his mind in order to escape seduction by the sirens, Elster shows how binding oneself to a course of action, despite periodic adjustments that appear better, is rational. In short, at least in some cases, the classical utilitarian model appears to generate inferior results compared with less discriminating techniques.[12]

The classical business example of this situation is the nervous buying and selling of stock by someone relatively new to the stock market. The greater the activity, the weaker the performance. A historical example might be the Susan B. Anthony dollar. Various sophisticated cost-benefit analyses strongly recommended minting the new dollar, and, as we know, its failure was unpredicted. The analyses neglected to consult consumer interest: People just didn't like it.

Adequacy as a Moral Theory

Utilitarianism as a theory of moral behavior still has strong support, even though it has also had its detractors over the years. In Chapter Two we touched upon some of the usual criticisms; they will not be reviewed here. Other recent criticisms, however, strike at the heart of important problems and are worth mentioning.

Both MacIntyre[13] and Pincoffs,[14] for example, express dismay over the utilitarian injunction always to judge the worth of an act by its consequences; for some acts, the good is internal to the act and is incommensurable with any external goods or consequences. We do some things simply because they are good in themselves, regardless of their consequences or external effects. (Think of promising, forms of friendship and devotion, commitment, honesty, service, and so on.) As a moral theory, utilitarianism encourages an instrumental regard for behavior that is probably inconsistent with at least some higher forms of human behavior. If the critics are correct, an adequate theory of decision making must allow for some acts that are simply expressions of character and are not good because of a successful comparison with other goods.

The Problem

Given the shortcomings of traditional utilitarian analysis just described, one of the more urgent tasks in business ethics is to provide a model of utilitarian reasoning that is closer to what has been learned in recent research and closer to managerial experience. We need a new view of utilitarian decision making that is:

1. A good descriptive theory — one that is at least compatible with how we see decision makers actually behaving

2. A promising, unbiased decision procedure

3. An acceptable theory of morality

This is asking for a great deal. The task is necessarily multidisciplinary and very difficult. In what follows, only a modest working proposal is presented.

A Taxonomy of Utilitarian Issues

One way to solve this problem is to admit at the outset that utilitarian decision situations demand multiple methods and that no single model of utilitarian thinking will best serve those various needs. Therefore, we challenge the common idea that a single decision procedure is best for every kind of utilitarian issue or that a single approach serves all purposes equally well. It would be a mistake to suppose that utilitarian issues are unitary, that is, that they are all of one type. This might be true only in the most abstract sense in which all utilitarian questions are resolved by selecting the alternative that is most satisfying. But as we shall see, even this is open to question. The differences among utilitarian issues are as important to attend to as the differences between utilitarian and formalistic reasoning, and recognizing those differences is essential for establishing the need for alternative models of utilitarian decision making.

In what follows, we identify three different types of utilitarian decision situations. There are probably more. We will examine how closely the classical maximizing view applies to each type. And we will see how the third type, especially, requires a different perspective on utilitarian thought from that supplied in the classical model.

The following typology is closely related to Mintzberg's analysis of the phases of decision making.[15] In that analysis, he developed a general descriptive model of decision making that consisted of three different general phases and various components of each phase. Any given decision situation may illustrate a particular "track" through the model. Thus, descriptively speaking, decision processes may be very different from each other. The three types of utilitarian issues to be discussed illustrate three different tracks in Mintzberg's model.

Type One: Entrepreneurial Utilitarianism

The first utilitarian issue turns on finding just the right alternative among many possible ones. It is a question of *what* to do, not *why*. Using Mintzberg's language, this type of utilitarian problem depends more significantly on the *development phase* than on the *selection phase* in that searching for or designing a solution to the problem is more important than evaluating or selecting one.[16] Following are examples of this type of utilitarian issue:

1. How do I face a group of employees who are disgruntled over recent management decisions?
2. How do I deal with the general public in defending the corporation's decision to relocate?
3. What general strategies should the corporation pursue in marketing its new line of products?
4. What can be done to increase the number of minority applicants for managerial positions at this corporation?
5. How can I redesign the flow of work in a particular section to reduce the rising friction among employees?

This kind of utilitarian issue is called *entrepreneurial* because it relies heavily on brainstorming or creative imagination. It focuses not on *why* one should do (or not do) something but *how* one should do something or *what* one should do. And there is no comparison of variables regarding their impact on preexisting alternatives. At best, a superior alternative is immediately recognized for what it is, and the comparison of variables is compressed, if not eliminated. The classical theory is appealed to in this case only in theory, with no practical relevance.

For this type of issue there is a heavy reliance on imagination, which generally forestalls the possibility of generating significant comparative utilitarian analysis of the classical type. Other than general brainstorming advice (such as on what, how, who, when, and where), little procedural help can be offered.

Therefore, for this kind of utilitarian issue, the classical theory clearly fails to give a descriptive account and provides little practical help, since processes of imagination can't be easily described. As a prescriptive theory, the traditional view may be more appropriate, since it offers an account of what it means to recognize a good idea when we see one. That is, when we suddenly hit upon a really good idea, what we mean by "really good" is that it promises to produce clearly superior results.

89

Type Two: Technocratic Utilitarianism

The second and third kinds of utilitarian issues appeal to the distinction between continuous and discrete alternatives. When the alternatives for action are continuous, this means that we have a wide range of actions to choose from, requiring close analysis. An example would be deciding how much money to spend on marketing a particular product: Any amount could be spent — from nothing to perhaps millions of dollars. By contrast, the third type of utilitarian issue, involving discrete alternatives, might be illustrated by a decision to replace or retain an employee.

This second type of utilitarian problem is similar to Mintzberg's description of the *technical analysis* phase of decision making: "In analysis . . . factual evaluation is carried out, generally by technocrats, followed by managerial choice by judgment or bargaining."[17] This mode of decision making is not common among strategic decision makers. Mintzberg reports that only 18 of 83 managers were observed to use the analytic approach.

To illustrate, the use of depletable natural resources is an issue of this type because it forces us to select the level of oil use in the form of gasoline, heating oil, and so on. The issue is not "Shall I use oil or not?" but rather "How much oil shall I use? — A little? A lot? How much?" Other examples of this kind of utilitarian issue include the following:

1. How much pollution is acceptable in our environment?
2. How much should one invest in capital improvements?
3. How much time should one give to community service?
4. How much money should I request for this year's budget?

This is one of the toughest kinds of utilitarian issues because although the alternatives for action are more or less all in mind, making fine discriminations among similar alternatives for action demands a level of analysis that is well honed and reliable. Such judgments tend to be "recipe-like": The greatest good for the greatest number depends on adjusting the precise levels of all contributing factors. Such problems are typical of those faced by public policy analysts. With unjustified optimism, President Lyndon Johnson once stated that utilitarian analysis in the form of planning-programming-budgeting-systems (PPBS) could solve highly complex problems and bring us closer to the Great Society:

> For example, how can we best help an underprivileged child break out of poverty and become a productive citizen? Should we concentrate on improving his education? Would it help more to spend the same funds for his food, or clothing, or medical care? Does the real answer lie in training his father for a job, or perhaps teaching his mother the principles of nutrition? Or is some combination of approaches most effective?[18]

The problem with this kind of decision making is the human limitations on foreseeing the consequences of actions. The temptation is to study continually and make frequent minor adjustments to policy as the consequences of previous adjustments become better known.

Although this second type of utilitarian issue probably generates a lot of criticism for producing arbitrary results, it is not the source of the other two problems we have identified. In fact, the classical utilitarian model probably does describe fairly well the intricate processes people use in trying to refine and adjust their approach to certain complex issues. And it is unlikely to prompt criticism as a moral theory because, again, the classical maximizing theory captures quite well the common human effort to adjust and arrange factors within our power to yield the best results.

Type Three: Managerial Utilitarianism

According to Minztberg, the "most favored" mode of evaluation and choice is what he calls the *judgment sub-phase*.[19] Here deliberation focuses more on the reasons or grounds for acting and less on the kinds of options that are available for action.

The alternatives for action generally consist of a small, closed set. Typical examples would include these:

1. Should I take the new job offer or stay in my present position?
2. Should I report the abuses of a colleague who is my friend?
3. Should I conform to traditional behavior that I think is unethical?
4. Should I produce and market a new product that may be dangerous to children?
5. To which of three candidates should I make a job offer?

For each of these questions, attention focuses not on what alternatives for action are possible but, instead, on the reasons one might have for acting. Discussions of utilitarian method in business ethics are typically modeled on this sort of issue, since it relates to comparing and aggregating reasons before selecting one alternative.

For this type of decision, the classical theory may be inferior to a new theory to be presented in the next section. Managers seldom, if ever, perform quantitative, comparative analyses as part of their deliberations on issues such as those previously described. And although they may still want to do what is best, they often do so for reasons that are merely adequate for deciding the issue. Thus, it would appear that what we need is an alternative to comprehensive utilitarian analysis that is compact, efficient, and reliable. We need a theory of adequate reason.

A Theory of Adequate Reason

To develop a new proposal concerning managerial forms of utilitarian decision making, we begin by focusing on a simple view of the kind of reasoning described in the discussion of managerial utilitarianism. Using the name for this type of reasoning, we will call it the *managerial model*.

This simple model presents only two alternatives (yes or no, do or don't, etc.) and depends for its resolution on multiple incommensurable variables. As with innumerable management cases, the factors relating to the resolution of the issue are not mutually compatible for analytic purposes. Thus, describing the prototypical case as turning on two or more incommensurable variables is realistic.

Rather than accept the traditional assumptions of utilitarianism, however, we turn the classical theory on its head and give them up. To assume that human beings can make comprehensive assessments of complex issues involving incommensurable variables and identify an optimal policy alternative is to assume human capacities of comparative judgment that research fails to observe. What is observed is managers selecting alternatives for what seem to be the *best available* reasons — seldom on the basis of all things considered (which is the *absence* of an explanation).

Who would be satisfied with a manager's account of what he or she had done that stated: "We chose to do this partly because of A, but also because of B, and a little bit of C"? Managers have strong reasons for wanting to be incisive; people like to hear clear reasons for action, not technical close calls. There is a natural human preference for explanations that are direct, clear-cut, penetrating, trenchant, and crisp. Where possible, managerial decisions of utility seek decisive reasons, which satisfy the human need for a clear explanation.

A New Set of Assumptions

Therefore, we boldly propose that utilitarian decision-making methods should fit their needs. And three types of utilitarian issues may each require a different approach. Consequently, a decision model that differs strongly from the classical utilitarian model will be employed for *managerial* needs. The assumptions underlying this new model replace the traditional assumptions and reflect recent indicated developments in management studies regarding decision processes and in moral theory. They are as follows:

1. **Adequate Reason.** Rather than demand that moral theory be perfect and that it secure the best results for the best reasons, we assume that to be moral is to select alternatives that are good enough for reasons that are also good enough. The traditional assumption that for every situation moral action is singular is merely an assumption; the alternative assumption adopted here is that for any given situation there may exist a number of moral actions, any of which may be selected for reasons that are adequate according to a theory of adequate reason (to be outlined shortly).

2. **Selective Analysis.** A more realistic description of traditional utilitarian analysis is that it pretends to be comprehensive while selecting for analysis only the most tractable variables. The new model allows quantitative analysis only where appropriate and allows other forms of nonquantitative comparison and selection as dictated by the nature of the issue. Comprehensiveness still applies as a requirement that a manager *consider* an issue from all perspectives, but *selection* of behavior does not demand that all reasons be simultaneously weighed according to some supposed common unit of reduction in order to search for the optimal alternative.

3. **Indeterminacy of Preferences.** The traditional theory assumes that reasons (as values or preferences) determine moral action and that one's reasons are givens that are consulted in order to select a proper course of action. The new model, by contrast, assumes that reasons are not givens; they may be selected as needed to justify behavior. In this system they have logical, but not temporal, priority. Regarding values or reasons as selected makes persons responsible not just for their actions but also for their reasons for acting. It attaches personal character to action and makes managers moral agents, not just moral technicians.

The new model, then, can be characterized as *taking responsibility for selecting morally satisfactory alternatives for adequate reasons.* In contrast to a recipe-like approach to questions of utility, where all relevant factors are allegedly given attention, the new assumptions bring to mind an "active ingredients" image of decision making, where choices turn on decisive factors that tip the scales in favor of some alternative. A step-by-step description of the new model might be as follows:

1. List the alternatives.
2. List the criteria.
3. Select the dominant criterion.
4. Select the alternative that best satisfies the dominant criterion.

This new model, of course, is strikingly different from the classical model of utilitarian decision making. Its acceptability depends entirely on the strength of the case that can be built for the existence of *dominant criteria* and knowing when they can be appealed to in lieu of the full range of criteria. The following section discusses this issue.

What Counts as Adequate Reasons

Managerial needs for decisiveness in questions of utility require beginning with the assumption that there is a single decisive reason for acting, which stands on its own in the face of criticism. The method simply consists of identifying the factor (or small set of factors) that carries the issue. The function of this assumption is to crystallize evaluative thinking around some value and focus attention on it by comparison with other values. Thus, the utilitarian issue is resolved not by a collective weighting of factors, but by the choice of (if possible) a single dominant or adequate factor. It is no less "open" than traditional utilitarianism, but it chooses rather than compares values. Following is an exploratory taxonomy of decisive factors.

1. ***Dominant Factors.*** Decisions made by movie critics illustrate this kind of factor. The decision is polar—yes (see the movie) or no (stay home)—and the reasons given often focus on some dominant positive or nega-

tive characteristic of the movie, such as a bad script, good acting, or exceptional special effects. A positive recommendation does not mean that this is the best possible movie to see; it simply means that it passes the test of being good enough. The task of the manager is to identify that factor and to convince others of its significance. In this respect, managers become teachers.

2. *An Uncompensated Factor.* For example, in deciding whether or not to accept a job offer, one might reason that (a) the salary increase is offset by the higher cost of living, that (b) one can always look forward to making new friends, even though the old friends will be hard to leave, and that (c) new forms of relaxation will replace old ones. But one might realize that one's teenage children do not understand these reasons and, indeed, can profit from relationships and opportunities that would be hard to replace when moving to a new location. Such a factor would be uncompensated, and therefore the decision could be described as turning on the decisive factor — in this example, the needs of one's children for a stable teenage experience. The uncompensated factor becomes an adequate reason in the sense that it is the sole significant variable.

3. *An Intrinsically Valued Factor.* Decisions are sometimes based on singular motives that in themselves are sufficient grounds for acting. In the case of love or service, for example, no admixture of motive is possible without calling into question the nature of the motive. Several managerial virtues may exemplify self-sufficient motives for acting, but two in particular are mentioned here:

    a. *Fidelity.* A business that remains in a community through tough times or an employee who remains with a project team despite attractive outside offers provides a good example of deciding on the basis of singularly important factors. Commitment, promise, fraternity, and loyalty are all examples of sufficient reasons for action on some occasions. This is why business decisions to relocate are sometimes described as motivated by narrow, selfish reasons.

b. **Civility.** Cooperation and trust are important components of any civilization. Individuals cannot be self-sufficient experts on all issues requiring evaluation. Sometimes they must entrust these responsibilities to others. Furthermore, some social rules are arbitrary and have little or no justification. As businesses abide by the canons of society, they participate in the civilization made possible by substantial cooperation in such matters. When businesses exploit the absence of monetary and legal penalties (with questionable advertising, high-pressure sales tactics, or general disregard for human flourishing), they undermine the cooperation upon which civilization is based.

This outline of decisive factors is not complete. A more comprehensive treatment would produce a theory of managerial virtues, among other things.

Justifying Managerial Utilitarianism

Although superficially the model of managerial utilitarianism may have a certain practical appeal, a convincing case for its worth must consist of an explication of its deeper advantages. The following discussion assesses its worth as a descriptive theory, as a useful decision-making tool, and as a moral theory.

Its Adequacy as a Descriptive Theory of Decision Making

The managerial model of decision making proposed here conforms more closely to recent research than the classic model. Soelberg, for example, found in a study of decision making that very few criteria were used to make decisions. He writes, "Not more than one or two of what we have called *prime* goal

97

attributes account for most of the observed variance."[20] Thus, at least one researcher reports the widespread use of what we have described as dominant criteria.

A second strength of the new model as a descriptive theory of human decision making is its denial that human beings make decisions on the basis of independent goals or values established prior to evaluation. Fahey reports that for many decisions the choice of goals and the selection of an alternative are not distinct components;[21] goals and alternatives appear to be equally matters of choice. James March describes this well:

> The argument that goal development and choice are in-dependent behaviorally seems clearly false. It seems to me perfectly obvious that a description that assumes goals come first and action comes later is frequently radically wrong. Human choice behavior is at least as much a process for discovering goals as for acting on them.[22]

By contrast, the new model proposed here assumes no weighting of factors and practically compels goal evaluation and selection by searching for the dominant or decisive factor. As Mitroff and Emshoff assert, "there really are no 'givens,' . . . there are only 'takens.'"[23]

The long-range effect of traditional utilitarian techniques is the abdication of managerial responsibility to technical decision making. The new model challenges the value-based determinism of traditional utilitarian thinking. It promotes reflection on the things that really count, and it brings utilitarian thinking more in line with responsible managerial behavior. Managers are persons who bear responsibility for important decisions made in organizations, and in doing so they accept responsibility for deciding what counts and what doesn't. Although they may tolerate others' differing values, their liberality does not dictate ethical relativism.

The traditional model, then, is unacceptable because ultimately it is nonmanagerial. Democracy is not administration; it is an alternative to administration. Part of what administration means is accepting responsibility to make decisions about what really counts and to ignore what doesn't, to choose directions, to promote a vision of a better arrangement of things, and to articulate those dominant aims to others. It also means ignoring distracting influences—arguments that may indeed be relevant but just don't make a big difference when it comes to making the decision. Managing is taking responsibility for what one chooses to set aside, as well as for what one chooses to attend to. Therefore, by encouraging the manager to focus on only those factors that really count, the new model appeals to an essential feature of managing and is, therefore, more attractive from a managerial perspective. This moves utilitarianism toward a classically objective position in which we trust managers or other leaders to lead wisely in the choice of direction while remaining tolerant of dissent.

Its Usefulness as a Reliable Method

Another reason for denying that comprehensiveness of analysis in utilitarian thinking is important is the realization that at least some steps taken to make an analysis more comprehensive also increase the arbitrariness of the conclusion. For example, the more factors one considers in a utilitarian analysis, the less likely it becomes that one will judge correctly the comparative contribution of each factor—especially when the factors are incommensurable. Examples of decision situations in which the comparison of relevant factors is highly arbitrary include the following:

1. Evaluating a written recommendation or report in terms of content, organization, style, timeliness, and so on

2. Judging the merit of faculty in terms of productivity, teaching, and service

3. Assessing a proposed business strategy in terms of all its impacts—on profits, the community, the environment, consumers, and so on

We don't need to include in this list the choice of a spouse to illustrate the point that trying to assess overall merit by assigning relative importance to various factors can be arbitrary, and that the attempt to treat some decisions in quasi-quantitative

99

terms can be at least impersonal and at most arbitrary, distorting, and even self-deceptive.

So, sometimes the heterogeneity or incommensurability of the factors can impede smooth analysis, but by selecting only those factors that are compatible with the form of analysis, traditional utilitarian analyses encourage arbitrary results. The proposed method, by contrast, doesn't invite decision makers to do more than they can be expected to do. Alternatives for acting that relate to incommensurable goals or values are presented as situations for choosing values rather than merely as alternatives. The choice of an alternative is really a choice of dominant or decisive value. As Lindblom argued almost 30 years ago, for traditional utilitarian analysis, "the inevitable exclusion of factors is accidental, unsystematic, and not defensible . . . while in the [new] branch method the exclusions are deliberate, systematic, and defensible."[24]

We must keep in mind, however, that if we try to adjust the classical model in order to accommodate the research we have cited, we might be giving too much credit to observed limitations in human behavior. Schwenk warns against excessive simplification in decision making, reminding us that human beings process information poorly when unassisted and that any recommended decision-making methods should stretch human capacities toward comprehension, not accommodate human limitations.[25]

These concerns are legitimate. I have tried to anticipate some of them here by restricting the new model's application to certain kinds of utilitarian decisions. A more complete theory of managerial decision making might examine more closely the link between quantitative analysis and decision situations, indicating those cases where traditional analysis is appropriate while being willing to distinguish those from others where a less comprehensive approach would serve better.

Its Propriety as a Moral Theory

The deficiencies of traditional utilitarianism as a moral theory are also made noticeable precisely in those cases where comprehensive analysis is most easily justified. In such cases, one must conclude that, on balance, many minor factors made the difference. But there are at least two things that are wrong with that kind of explanation from a managerial point of view. First, it is too defensible. It hides justification for the decision in a lot of "utilitarian clutter," and it inoculates itself against any kind of easily focused criticism. As Karl Popper would put it, the strongest and most reasonable judgments are those that are most easily examined.[26] But an account that appeals to a large set of reasons or factors points to nothing in particular that might have made the difference. It is, therefore, less easily scrutinized, and therefore less decisive and more arbitrary.

The second thing that is wrong with an explanation appealing to a comprehensive set of factors is related to the first: Where justifications are less accessible to close criticism, they also facilitate rationalization. That is, they are more easily manipulated post hoc to generate results supporting some preconceived outcome or personal bias. To reduce the likelihood of the manager's confusing precision with a facade of expertise, one must be ready to regard utilitarian decisions resting on a comprehensive set of factors as significantly arbitrary and subject to the influence of increasing subjectivity — even deception.

Furthermore, classical utilitarianism presupposes the obsolescence of managerial virtues. According to the traditional model, the only managerial virtue is technical competence. There is no appeal to courage, fidelity, civility, or any other virtues indicating that one takes personal responsibility for the decision. Even benevolence, the prime goal of traditional utilitarian analyses, is a product of the method, not of the decision maker. According to the model proposed here, however, the presence of managerial virtue can be regarded as an adequate reason for action under certain circumstances; thus, the new model is more compatible with a theory of managerial virtues and with our common tendency to attribute moral grounds for acting to managerial discretion.

Finally, the new model replaces the traditional maximization criterion with the beginning of a theory of reasons. Thus, moral competence no longer simply refers to mechanical proficiency in comparing values, but to the ability to select appropriate reasons.

Shortcomings of the New Model

The managerial utilitarianism model being proposed in this book has several virtues, but it also exhibits at least one shortcoming. The problem that seems most significant is the possibility that the new model is myopic and encourages the pursuit of merely proximate ends by persons unwilling to extend themselves in the process of evaluating the relative contributions of variables. That is, instead of deciding what factors really count, one might simply select the factor or factors that count for the individual. It is possible, for example, that in focusing on the decisive factors, one carries decisiveness and practicality too far and merely adopts a selfish orientation, or the prevailing ideology, or a shortsighted perspective when a broader consideration of factors might facilitate a more ethical study of the issue. Thus, if the new model of managerial utilitarianism is to be adopted, it must provide some assurances against premature closure or merely habitual or selfish selection of decisive factors. In short, it must fight excessive proximity by balancing the natural tendency of the new model to *focus* on decisive reasons with a set of reminders that promote an open consideration of disparate elements. As Elbing advises, "Ask yourself a large number of specific questions and look for patterns in the answers."[27] So, we will look for a pattern of decisiveness amid a wholly open array of questions. The array of questions will act as a check on excessive proximity. Those checks might consist of reminders of the forms excessive proximity can take:

1. *Spatial (or Personal) Proximity.* This is the tendency to regard one's own preferences as more important than those of others. It represents the natural tendency toward selfishness.

2. *Temporal Proximity.* This refers to the emphasis on short-term goals over long-term goals. Marx, in particular, was critical of utilitarianism's apparent bias toward conservatism. He thought that Bentham's theory of utility was "a mere apology of what exists."[28]

3. *Sociocultural Proximity.* This is the tendency to adopt

as one's dominant values the views and preferences of a particular gender, race, creed, neighborhood, or other group.

4. *Species Proximity.* Utilitarianism has long been known for its insistence on considering only human values as relevant for analysis, to the exclusion of nonhuman or inanimate values or needs. Tribe, for example, calls attention to the homocentric tendency of policy analysts in establishing environmental policies and regulations.[29]

In requiring managers to make judgments of utility by focusing on the decisive factors, the proposed model may be encouraging excessive proximity, especially among administrators unaccustomed to extending themselves. Furthermore, a variety of widely regarded unethical behaviors can be seen as attempts to coerce decision making, such as bribes, threats, offers of personal favors, perks, and so on. Each of these can become a decisive reason for acting unless the tendency toward excessive proximity can be checked.

If excessive proximity is a problem of overreduction for the new model of managerial utilitarianism, the model more than compensates for this by considerably decreasing a far more serious reductionist problem that infects the traditional approach, namely, the kinds of distortions that accompany analytic reductions of multiple variables to a single proxy variable (which is usually money).

Under traditional utilitarian procedures, the requirement that multiple factors' contributions be measured and compared compels the use of a single unit of comparative value—usually money. But in this mode of analysis, money serves as an *instrumental* variable, in theory representing the comparative value of any number of other variables, some of which may be intrinsically valuable. Reducing the value of each variable to money and using money as a proxy variable encourages the presumption that money itself is to be highly valued (perhaps because of its analytic versatility or its role as a universal standard of value). But exchangeability on paper does not imply real exchangeability: Learning to play the piano, for example, cannot be accomplished merely through an exchange of money; it also requires effort through time. Furthermore, overvaluing money might distract us from considering the import of other values. For example, if one asked the typical business student why he or she was studying business, the typical response would be, "To get a job." And, of course, the reason for getting a job is to make money—and the more the better. But relatively few business students have bothered to ask themselves what would *really* make them happy. A carefully considered answer to that question might point to some goals that require comparatively little money or even to another field of study or skill development. Supposing money to represent value in general and to be roughly translatable into other values (when those values are eventually perceived) tends to postpone (or even eliminate) the perception of those other values until it is too late. Thus, money takes on an exaggerated importance with respect to other values, due in large part to its analytic function as a proxy variable.

Kurt Vonnegut's classical novel *Player Piano* carries to an extreme the social implications of the reductionist tendencies of traditional utilitarian policy analytic techniques. It describes a society that has lost touch with all but the most superficial values and that finds it increasingly difficult to convince itself that its traditional measures and indices of satisfaction and happiness are faithful to human ends. Vonnegut speaks of our own society and its tendency to exaggerate the exchangeability of goods, forgetting that though other goods *may* be similarly valued, they are not easily exchanged.[30]

So, although the new model of managerial utilitarianism proposed in this book admits to sharing certain practical difficulties with traditional techniques, at least it discourages the kinds of reductions and distortions that befall the latter. In requiring the decision maker to focus on the smallest set of decisive factors, the need to smooth over any discontinuities among variables is significantly reduced, and the use of proxy variables such as money is discouraged.

The practical assessment of traditional utilitarian procedures recommends an alternative utilitarian approach to be used in managerial situations where measurement, quantitative comparison, and comprehensive analysis are less important than convenience, cost, and decisiveness. The alternative approach assumes that comprehensiveness of analysis wastes a lot of energy on dubious and sometimes needless analytic precision, and it justifies its decisions not in the contours of a complex study, but in the intuition and articulation of a small set of decisive reasons. One does not have to be quantitative to be rational; in fact, as we have seen, quantification applied to ethical thinking sometimes causes irrationalities of its own.

One of the distinctive features of this new form of utilitarian analysis is its shifting of responsibility to the decision maker. And for some kinds of ethical issues, this is particularly important. "Commons" problems, for example, defy practical resolution under standard utilitarian rationalism: Overseas bribery, military sales to foreign nations, trafficking in drugs, and even defacing roadside scenery with billboards and other advertising are all typified by the fact that no one wants to be the "sacrificial lamb" who breaks the cycle of such business activities. But requiring managers to reflect upon what really counts at least focuses responsibility where it needs to be to resolve such problems—on the manager. With respect to commons problems, Pastin says, "we must let responsibility back in if organizations are to function ethically and effectively.... Responsibility is the only effective force because it breaks the commons gridlock of interests. We must *create* responsibility."[31]

One of the ways to promote responsible action among managers is to help them to strengthen the link between their own decisions and society's well-being. Often what needs to be done in situations is clear, but getting persons to accept responsibility for doing it is the problem. By focusing judgments of utility on the possibility of decisive reasons, managers build personal responsibility for action and increase the likelihood of overcoming serious problems that might otherwise be impossible to resolve.

Summary of Key Concepts

1. The three classical assumptions of utilitarianism are:
   a. Maximization of good results
   b. Measurement and comparison of goods to select the most attractive alternative
   c. The "givenness" of people's preferences, which are not themselves evaluated

2. Classical utilitarianism is inadequate for managerial purposes as:
   a. A descriptive theory, because managers often make decisions based on reasons that seem to be good enough, not for reasons that are the best
   b. A reliable method, because nonquantitative factors are usually given less consideration, thus distorting analysis
   c. A moral theory, because it promotes the attitude that no action is good in itself — only good for some end or other

3. There are at least three types of utilitarian issues:
   a. Entrepreneurial, which requires imaginative solutions
   b. Technocratic, which selects some action from a range of available incremental steps
   c. Managerial, which makes decisions for what seem to be the best available reasons

4. Managerial utilitarianism is founded on three new assumptions:
   a. Reasons do not need to be perfect — only good enough or adequate.
   b. Decisions do not need to be accounted for in terms of all relevant factors — only those factors (usually one or two) that make the difference.
   c. Our preferences are not given; as we study issues, we may find that our preferences change or become more clearly known to us.

5. What counts as an adequate reason for acting can be a variety of things, including (a) dominant factors, (b) uncompensated factors, and (c) intrinsically valued factors.

6. This new theory of managerial utilitarianism provides a better description of how managers make decisions of utility. In some respects, it is a more reliable method. And it may even be a superior moral theory.

7. The chief danger of managerial utilitarianism is its tendency to accept reasons that are too selfish or too narrowly focused. It must be constantly on guard against excessive proximity of various kinds in seeking good reasons for action.

Questions and Exercises

1. Every now and then, someone does a study to decide which city in the United States is best.
   a. What criteria would you use?
   b. How would you measure and compare those criteria?
   c. Which criteria are most important? Least important?
   d. Would you ever feel convinced that such a study had done a good job? Would you trust the study? Why or why not?
   e. Could you feel certain that you had listed all the criteria and ranked them correctly?
   f. How does this study illustrate the traditional utilitarian analytic techniques, and how might a more decisive approach be more appropriate in a given instance?
   g. In making this kind of study, would it be fair to say that people are learning as much about their preferences as about their favorite cities?

2. One of the best examples of traditional utilitarian techniques applied in awkward ways are the product comparisons in each issue of *Consumer Reports*. For example, the October 1986 issue compared 106 ready-to-eat breakfast cereals. An index score ranging from a high of 78 (Quaker Puffed Wheat) to a low of 18 (Oh's Honey Grahams) was constructed by measuring and comparing the amounts of five ingredients: fiber, protein, sugar, sodium, and fat.
   a. What kind of utilitarian decision does this represent?
   b. What problems can you perceive in the index scores?
   c. Were any factors left out in computing the index scores?
   d. Are there any situations where the choice of a breakfast cereal turns on a decisive factor?
   e. Is the average situation likely to turn on decisive factors, or might one profit from the index scores?

3. Bring your favorite consumer comparison to class and evaluate its formula for comparing products.

4. Think of how difficult the teacher's job is when grading essays. A large number of factors are involved in produc-

ing a work of quality: sticking to the issue, writing articulately, good organization, imagination and creativity, reasonability, persuasiveness, grammar and mechanics, and other important elements. How does an instructor take into consideration all these different factors when evaluating an essay? As and Fs are easy to recognize, but how does one distinguish between Bs and Cs?

    a. How does this issue illustrate the problem of traditional utilitarian analysis?

    b. How could the new model described in this chapter be used, if at all, to make the grading problem easier and more trusted?

5. Consider your own career plans. What factors are most important (beginning with salary versus genuine interest in the job)?

6. The Susan B. Anthony dollar was predicted by every congressional analysis to save the government about $35 million a year, due primarily to its average life of 15 years compared to the average life of a dollar bill, which is 1.5 years. In addition, several women's groups strongly supported the measure. In 1979 three-quarters of a billion Susan B. Anthony dollars were let loose upon the land. Today we have no such dollar.

    a. What happened?

    b. What does this failure to predict illustrate — poor method or poor application?

    c. When circumstances allow, policy changes are preceded by pilot studies. What can pilot studies do that classical utilitarian analysis cannot?

    d. How might the story of the Susan B. Anthony dollar illustrate the matter of falsifiability, as described by Popper?

7. How is the majority vote a form of utilitarian evaluation? How many factors are represented in such a process? Is it efficient? How much does a majority vote tell us about the grounds for selecting one candidate or proposal over another?

8. Who must bear the burden of airport noise? Several decades ago, when Lindberg Field was first built in San

Diego, California, it was well away from the center of town. Few aircraft used the field, and those that did were not particularly noisy by today's standards. A mile or two down the flight path of departing aircraft is a peninsula of land called Point Loma. Over the years, people built houses on Point Loma, thinking that aircraft traffic there was not a great inconvenience. No one could have foreseen, however, the volume of air traffic and the noise of modern jets. In the 1980s, the residents of Point Loma came to regard the airport noise as a cost borne by them without compensation. From a utilitarian perspective, should the environment of Point Loma residents continue to be sacrificed for other goods benefiting the larger San Diego community?

9. One very important utilitarian issue is that of *comparable worth*. That is, how does one compare the value of jobs that are significantly dissimilar, with confidence that the salaries attached to those jobs are reasonable? For example, should a secretary's salary be higher or lower than that of a truck driver? Thinking of this general issue, answer the following questions:

   a. What are the various ways in which jobs can differ from each other?

   b. Which of the factors listed in (a) are most important? Can you rank the factors in terms of their relative importance?

   c. Given your answers to (a) and (b), do you think classical utilitarian decision-making procedures will generate confidence in any proposed solution?

   d. Given that women's salaries traditionally have been about 60 percent of men's salaries for similar work, would it be fair to say that gender has been a dominant factor? Is this a case of excessive proximity? What kind?

   e. What factors other than gender might serve alone as adequate reasons for salaries?

10. Until recently, Eastern Airlines had the policy of using lost luggage temporarily to train dogs to sniff out bombs in airline luggage. Lost luggage was flown to the training lo-

cation, dynamite was inserted in some pieces, and dogs were brought in to sniff out the dynamite. On one occasion, the trainers forgot to remove one of the sticks of dynamite before the lost luggage was returned to its owner. Upon opening his luggage, the owner was at a loss to explain the dynamite, and the story went to the newspapers. With no other way to explain the phenomenon, Eastern went public with its policy.

a. From a classical utilitarian perspective, does it make sense to use lost luggage for a day or two to train dogs?

b. Are any ethical principles being violated in doing so? How does one assign utility to the keeping (or violating) of ethical principles?

C H A P T E R

6

Practical Formalism

From Chapters Three and Four we learned that both utilitarians and formalists historically have claimed to possess an exclusive decision procedure in ethics. With less confidence than the historical proponents of these positions, however, authors of typical business-society texts generally present both views as "approaches" or "orientations" in ethics without emphasizing their *methodological* natures. Furthermore, the treatment of the two views is seldom symmetrical. Of the two, utilitarianism receives the fuller presentation, probably because it bears such a close resemblance to forms of thinking with which business students are already familiar and because it is deceptively straightforward. It is often characterized as a kind of democratic cost-benefit analysis. And although the procedural shortcomings of utilitarian analysis are both severe and well known, as we have seen, utilitarianism still enjoys wide appeal and acceptance as a useful approach to business-society issues.

Textual reviews of the formalist position, however, are less satisfactory. Without exception, presentations of Kant's position suffer from vagueness and from the high level of abstraction inherent in Kant's work. The introduction to formalistic reasoning in Chapter Three is typical of such presentations. Most authors, for example, mention Kant's categorical imperative and refer to such notions as universalization and a priori

113

judgments, but the complexity and abstraction of these concepts hamper their application to concrete cases. (Kant himself was so concerned about the alleged impracticality of his work that he wrote a short essay titled "On the Old Saw: That May Be Right in Theory But It Won't Work in Practice."[1])

Attempts to reduce the level of abstraction in formalism generally take one of two courses:

1. *Discussions of the Moral Importance of Motives.*[2] This approach, however, overlooks the fact that many business-society issues do not turn on questions of motive but, more often, on conceptual questions relating to responsibility, fairness, duty, equality, and so on. Typical questions are "What am I responsible for?", "What would be the fair thing to do in this situation?", and "Should I treat my employees with equality or recognize superior performance?".

2. *Conversions of Kantian Formalism Into a Theory of Individual Rights.*[3] This approach, however, merely disguises the former vaguenesses under a more familiar jargon (rights instead of duties) and restricts the range of application of the method. If formalism only decides questions of rights, other issues regarding the nature of an action, distribution of resources, and situational differences will be less accessible.

The conversion of an abstract philosophical formalism into a more usable form has not been accomplished, and in no case is formalism examined in terms of its methodological contribution. Unless a better job can be done in explicating formalist ethics, its impotence for business issues is secured, and students of business administration may, by default, revert to narrowly utilitarian perspectives.

The purpose of this chapter, then, is to develop a less abstract and more useful account of ethical formalism as it applies to business-society issues. Its chief virtue consists in the fact that it accounts for a wide range of arguments and perspectives found in the business ethics literature.

The Method in Detail

The method to be described does not derive from any philo-sophical position or abstract argumentation; it is simply a de-scription of the dominant form of ethical argumentation in the business ethics literature other than abundant examples of utilitarian thinking. What follows is more or less a complete description of that form of reasoning. But in its natural con-text, it seldom if ever occurs in its complete form; instead, one discovers fragments of the method — a line of thought partially developed, a counterpoint, a modestly supported conclusion — as with examples of utilitarian thinking, which are equally brief and fragmented in each instance of their use. Gathered and organized, the fragments of formalistic reasoning com-prise the general method to be described.

The method is basically this: *(1) The law (moral or legal) is developed incrementally through a cyclical process of (2) articulating principles that are (3) intuited in actual or conceived cases in order to give application to a (4) constitution-like set of core values or*

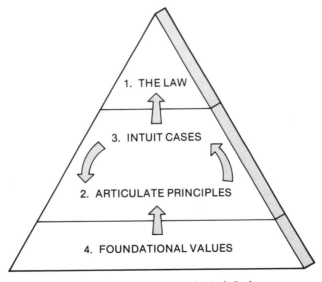

The Formalist Methodological Cycle

ideals. That is, advances in ethical thinking, as in legal systems, occur case by case as we learn the limits of the application of our principles. The main features of the method will now be discussed in detail.

Foundational Values

This method begins with the assumption that legal and moral systems must be founded upon sets of prime values that generate and guide the construction of the systems upon which they are based. We can look to several sources for the values that underlie business life in the United States. Gerald Cavanagh lists the following values: achievement and success, activity and work, efficiency and practicality, moral orientation and humanitarianism, freedom, equality, patriotism, material comfort, external conformity, and rationality and measurement.[4] John Rohr lists freedom, equality, and property as the three dominant "regime values."[5] The Bill of Rights, of course, is also an example of the "constitutional" function of values as a foundation for ethical and legal systems. In large organizations, a similar function is served by such things as professional and ethical codes, corporate policies, and employee handbooks.

Issues in the business-society literature often turn on the choice of values in the foundational set. Discussions about affirmative action programs often turn on the assumption concerning the degree of human self-determination, control, and responsibility. When a person argues, for instance, that "the most qualified person deserves the job" or that "hard work pays off," he or she is making assumptions about the nature of self-determination and the distribution of employment opportunities, respectively. One can just as easily point to the assumptions that lie at the heart of environmental issues or international business problems. The fact that these values function as givens in ethical formalism is in part indicated by the difficulties we have in agreeing on the solutions to problems that turn on those values, such as remedies for discrimination and environmental pollution. As givens, they can only be assumed, not argued for.

Intuiting Cases

Perhaps the most important component of formalistic method is the intuition of cases, for it is on the basis of cases that the moral law is tested, justified, applied, and modified. The kinds of cases that are frequently found in business ethics literature include, but are not limited to, the varieties that will now be discussed.

Extreme Cases   Extreme cases are productive to consider, since they often illustrate principles that can be used to bracket further examination. For example, the environmental issue of how to manage dwindling world supplies of oil is constrained on one end by unacceptable gluttony and on the other by taking the rights of future generations too seriously. DeGeorge writes,

> [Oil] . . . is a nonrenewable resource and is limited in quantity. How many generations in the future are we to allow to have present claim to it? Obviously, if we push the generations into the unlimited future and divide the oil deposits by the number of people, we each end up with the right to a gallon or a quart or a teaspoon or a thimblefull. So we must reconstrue the claim to refer to the practical use of oil.[6]

With extreme cases, we can learn to explain or justify policies or forms of thought that often build an undeserved reputation for rigid and inflexible formalist (or absolutist) thinking. Such cases can be employed to show how standing by one's principles may sometimes consist of rather moderate positions, by comparison with more extreme stances that could have been taken.

Counterfactual Cases   Counterfactuals invite us to consider cases where the facts are different from, or perhaps even opposite to, those of the original case under consideration. By juggling the facts, we can begin to discover which are important and which are not. For example, Judith Jarvis Thomson considers arguments against reverse discrimination

117

in employment by changing some facts that we are accustomed to stereotyping:

> To turn to particular cases, it might happen that the black applicant is middle class, the son of professionals, and has had the very best in private schooling; or that the woman applicant is plainly the product of feminist upbringing and encouragement. Is it proper, much less required, that the black woman be given preference over a white male who grew up in poverty, and has to make his own way and earn his encouragements?[7]

According to this case, histories of encouragement or hardship seem more relevant criteria for hiring than skin color. Thomson ultimately rejects this argument on other grounds but does give it credit for being what seems to her the most powerful argument against preferential hiring.

Analogies and Metaphors Analogies and metaphors are often helpful in appealing to intuitions that are otherwise masked by the complexities of real cases. Albert Carr, for example, provides insight into business negotiations and other competitive relations by suggesting that business bluffing is like playing poker: No one tells the truth about what they have in their hand, but then no one is expected to. The same is true, he says, in business: Business persons are not completely honest with each other; but then, no one is expected to be. The differences from, as well as the similarities with, poker provide genuine ethical insight into a variety of business behaviors.[8]

Similarly, when Peter Drucker objects to identifying Lockheed's actions in the famous bribery case as "paying a bribe," he uses another analogy to persuade us of the alleged naming error:

> There is no speech, article, book or conference on business ethics, for instance, which does not point an accusing finger in great indignation at Lockheed for giving in to a Japanese airline company that extorted money as a prerequisite to considering the purchase of

Lockheed's faltering L-1011 jet plane. There was very little difference between Lockheed's paying the Japanese and the pedestrian in New York's Central Park handing his wallet over to a mugger. Yet no one would have considered the pedestrian to have acted "unethically."[9]

Drucker's analogy is designed to excuse Lockheed's behavior under pressure. A corporation facing extortion, he says, can be like a pedestrian facing a mugger: Neither should be judged to be unethical for handing over the money. Whether this analogy succeeds or fails depends on the tightness of the analogy under further examination.

Karl Weick invites us to "mutate metaphors" when thinking about organizations. He reviews a variety of literature that portrays organizations as anarchies, seesaws, space stations, garbage cans, and so on. "Metaphors," he writes, "enable people to predicate characteristics that are unnamable. It's frequently impossible for people to find the appropriate words; when faced with this impasse, people use metaphors to portray what they cannot portray literally."[10] Describing a business expense, for example, as a *grease payment* is ethically different from identifying it as a *bribe*; and yet, the metaphor of maintaining organizational machinery in "working order" brings some legitimacy to the behavior that the word *bribe* does not.

Reverse Cases Velasquez reports that reversibility is an important aspect of Kantian formalism.[11] It requires us to consider the acceptability of acting on reasons that others could also appeal to as a basis for how they treat us. Thus, reverse cases are designed to promote empathy and open-mindedness with respect to all sides of an issue.

Reversibility is implicit in management decisions to undergo whatever requirements are imposed on employees: cuts in pay, polygraph tests, and so on. It is critical for producing an awareness of the repressed position of disadvantaged minorities and women and for eradicating the narrow-minded forms of thinking that underlie discrimination in the workplace.

Arguments appealing to the possibility of reversibility are

at the center of issues relating to the use of animals in research and testing. Descriptions of the confined life of veal calves, the draize test (where rabbits' eyes are used to test the irritability of products destined for human use), experimental procedures, and so on are designed to evaluate the morality of such practices by inviting us to consider being treated that way ourselves. Deciding whether such processes are "humane" is a linguistic reminder to consider the reverse case. At the very least, the homocentric and egocentric perspectives distort wider obligations and sympathies by flattening them into aspects of self-interest, distortions that reverse cases are often used to prevent.[12]

In July 1987, a Los Angeles judge sentenced an apartment landlord, known to his tenants as the "Ratlord," to live in one of his apartments for a month in order to pay for his failure to keep up his apartments. Perhaps the judge was trying to compel reverse thinking in a situation where it was pivotal for moral thought.

Precedent   Perhaps the most useful case to consider is the one that establishes a precedent for an action. Since consistency is a necessary condition for the application of formalistic principles, showing that similar situations in the past were resolved consistently becomes a powerful argument for similar action in the case under consideration, in the absence of special circumstances.

For example, Christopher Stone's assertion that trees and other natural objects should be given legal standing is supported historically by the granting of expanded rights or legal status to women, blacks, and corporations. In all such cases, the initial proposal to confer rights on some new entity must have sounded laughable, but it was followed at length by recognition and acceptance. Thus, there are precedents for granting rights to nonhuman objects.[13]

So, precedent is conservative; but it often conserves more than it should, serving as an excuse for undisciplined behavior. How often do we hear business executives justify errant acts with the statement "Everyone else is doing it. Why can't I?"

Counterexamples Raising cases with the opposite effect of precedent is the function of counterexamples. This may be the most common use of cases in ethical discussion. Counterexamples appeal to one's moral intuitions in challenging the generality of principles or generalizations by raising a case where application of the maxim is counterintuitive.

Examples are numerous. Von Hayek uses a counterexample when he objects to Galbraith's claim that the majority of (producer-generated) wants experienced by individuals in society are neither urgent nor important. In other words, Galbraith claims that because advertising is so influential, consumers' buying preferences reflect transient wants more than urgent needs. But Von Hayek reminds us that an appreciation for great literature, music, and painting is also generated in part by the producers and promoters of such products of civilization, yet we do not regard them as unimportant. So, Von Hayek's discussion of music, literature, and painting is meant to serve as a counterexample to Galbraith's claim that producer-generated wants are always unimportant.[14]

Archetypal Cases Differences among the major views of the relation between business and society are due not to differences in principle but to differing intuitions regarding the nature and basic conditions of human life. Often the most foundational principles rely on archetypal cases for their development.

John Rawls is a classic example. His highly controversial *difference principle* is grounded in an appeal to consider the circumstances (called the *original position*) where the originators of society impartially posit the rules of social organization in complete ignorance of their own status in that society. This archetypal case emphasizes rationality, the desire for liberty, and risk aversion.[15]

By contrast, Robert Nozick's fundamental intuitions regarding the same matters emphasize self-interest, individualism, and acceptance of risk. Similar to John Locke's *state of nature*, Nozick's view of social development emphasizes the individual acquisition and transfer of goods. Both Rawls and Nozick draw heavily from their archetypal cases in generating the principles of social organization and defining the status of business institutions in society.[16]

Additional examples of archetypal thinking might include Kurt Vonnegut's *Player Piano*, nuclear war scenarios, Adam Smith's pin factory, the prisoner's dilemma, Mandeville's *The Grumbling Hive*, and so on.

Articulating Principles

The second step in formalistic reasoning involves the articulation of the intuitive features in the cases that are relevant for justifying or adjusting the maxim that comprise our moral law. The kinds of characteristics articulated in this step are frequent in business ethics literature and include, but are not limited to, the examples that follow.

Distinctions   One conceptual objective of formalistic analysis is the making of distinctions. Thinking that two situations are the same when they are really different can lead to ethical mistakes. Several business-society issues, for example, turn on the need to distinguish between related descriptions of an act:

1. Bribes and "grease payments"
2. Lying and bluffing
3. "Bait and switch" and "lost leaders"
4. Benign and invidious discrimination
5. Corporate trade secrets and marketable employee skills
6. Employee freedom of expression and disloyalty to one's employer
7. Acting on inside information and acting on publicly available information
8. Deceptive advertising and customary "puffery"

Distinctions are often necessary to avoid equivocation in ethical contexts. For example, the often-seen bumper sticker "If guns are outlawed, only outlaws will have guns," although a powerful piece of rhetoric, is flawed in several ways. One of these consists of the equivocation on the word *outlaw*. Attending to the attributes of the two different uses of the word helps to clarify the ethical argument submerged in the rhetoric. In the first case, *outlaw* means "prohibit," and smoothly functioning societies require a large set of such prohibitions. In the second case, *outlaw* refers to persons who commit socially dysfunctional acts. Obviously, most prohibitions are not socially dysfunctional. Therefore, part of the appeal of the bumper sticker turns on an equivocation that carries rhetorical appeal but little logical force. And unpacking the attributes of concepts, even when apparently equivocal, can lead to ethically significant results.

A second example of making a distinction in order to avoid equivocating comes from an insight by Stanley Benn into the nature of the influence of advertising upon consumers. Benn argues that there has been a shift in the meaning of the word *satisfaction*:

> I may get satisfaction from contemplating a picture or reading a novel, but this is not necessarily because a desire to look at a picture has been satisfied. On the other hand, if I desire X and get X my desire is satisfied but it may give me no satisfaction . . . . [And] . . . if my desires were simply the contrivance of persuadors, they might very well be like this . . . . If this is true, advertising that presents consumption as a self-fulfilling activity . . . is essentially corrupting in that it promotes a misconception of the nature of man.[17]

So, arguing that advertising promotes consumer satisfaction by increasing the number of desires to be satisfied really turns on an equivocal use of the word *satisfaction*, which is laid bare by an analysis of the different attributes.

Thus, this view grants ethical status to what might sometimes be regarded as verbal exercises. But as these examples have shown, at least some semantic disputes are not merely disputes over words.

Generalizations   A second conceptual tool is the making of generalizations. When produced in a normative context, generalizations take the form of principles, rules, policies, reg-

123

ulations, and guidelines. Such examples are so plentiful that there is little need here to illustrate them. However, the most common error in making generalizations is worth discussing briefly. This is the *hasty generalization*, which results in stereotypes and simplistic thinking.

For example, Milton Friedman's famous claim that "the social responsibility of business is to increase its profits" is persuasive, in part because of its simplicity.[18] Like most simplistic notions, however, it presumes to increase one's understanding, not by inquiring after deeper and richer insights but by reducing what needs to be understood to a bare minimum. Such a claim is evaluated by laying bare the full range of attributes of executive responsibility. What results is a fairly complex set of responsibilities, interests, and freedoms that seems to pay a high price in reducing clarity, and yet it buys considerable more accuracy.[19]

Practical Administrative Application

Although the skeletal development of formalistic reasoning presented earlier seems simple enough, the logical relation between each kind of case and what it contributes to a more refined principle is much more complex and requires much more examination than can be given here. This will constitute an important part of legal and administrative scholarship in the future. But we can give some indications of how formalistic reasoning is a feature of typical administrative decisions.

From the administrative point of view, situations requiring formalistic reasoning typically arise as a challenge to an existing rule or policy. The thoughtful administrator must decide either to apply and enforce the rule or policy or to modify the rule in order to allow for the new kind of case being considered. In doing so, the administrator will ask the following questions:

1. Does the proposed action have any precedent?
2. What situations might be analogous to the one under consideration, and how does the rule apply in those cases?

3. Is the proposed action extreme, or are there other possibilities, more extreme still, that are clearly disallowed?

4. Would one be willing to have the rule applied to oneself as well?

5. What kinds of problems might be caused by modifying the rule to allow for the proposed action? Would the new rule bring about greater consistency or greater confusion or trouble? That is, are there any counterexamples to a modification of the rule?

6. Suppose that the case was different. Are there any variations on the facts of this case that might make a difference?

7. Are there any overarching general principles to which one can appeal for guidance?

The kind of thinking required to answer such provoking questions is comprehensive and, therefore, highly imaginative. The practical problem in doing formalistic ethical analysis, then, goes beyond being aware of the kinds of reasons and arguments that lead to universalizability and requires some kind of template for systematically loosening up and expanding one's thinking so that answers to the preceding questions can be discovered.

One way of accomplishing this task is to take the essential components of a business ethics issue and explode them, looking for insights. For example, if we examine the issue of whether human embryos should be transplanted for a profit, we identify the following four essential components: human, embryo, transplant, and profit. To explode each of the words means to list any other word that comes to mind that is related to that word, either positively or negatively. For example:

human	*embryo*	*transplant*	*profit*
nonhuman	kidney	freeze	gift
cows	hair	store	rent
plants	heart	graft	tax
baboon		transfuse	warranty
virus		destroy	

And so on. What happens in the course of performing this somewhat systematic explosion of ideas relating to the issue at hand is the recognition of a variety of questions that need attention.

1. If the transplant were not for profit, would that make a difference?

2. We routinely transplant cow embryos into mother cows. What difference does it make if we perform this operation on human women?

3. We have been transplanting plant material for years by grafting, cross-pollinating, and so on. Again, should the fact that the material is human make any difference?

4. If human embryo transplantation were allowed for profit, would associated market concepts like *guarantee, warranty, tax status, rentability,* and so on also apply?

The answers to these questions provide precedent, counterexamples, and all the other arguments that together comprise a formalistic response to the question of whether an action is ethical.

What remains to be done in this investigation of formalistic reasoning is a task that is too large for this book: an inquiry into just how the various cases and forms of reasoning previously identified interact with each other to produce general arguments or positions. If we examined a complex issue such as the ethical foundations of reverse discrimination, for instance, we would find a vast collection of cases, distinctions, and generalizations employed on either side of the issue. To my knowledge, no one has looked at the general structure of such arguments or positions to see what are considered strengths or weaknesses. Without such an understanding, complex issues such as a national policy on discrimination will be resolved only through attrition as people tire of pursuing their causes. But ethics is more than politics, and there is urgent need in the field of business ethics for a better understanding of the collective rationality of the components of formalistic reasoning previously identified.

The Link to Kant

The heart of Kantian ethics is the notion of the categorical imperative. Kant provides several versions, of which the best known in this: "Act only according to that maxim by which you can at the same time will that it should become a universal law."[20] As innumerable authors have noted, the methodological essence of the categorical imperative is the requirement that maxims of action be universalizable. Kant's attempts to illustrate universalizing in proscribing suicide, lying, idleness, and indifference toward others' hardships are highly problematic.[21] And even the most recent attempts to clarify the notion of universalizing have achieved only moderate success.[22]

The method described in this chapter can be described as Kantian because it provides a reasonable, useful account of universalizing. From this point of view, universalizing a maxim consists in testing the plausibility of the maxim against the universe of all conceivable relevant situations. In other words, the universality of a maxim or principle is established by subjecting it to successive case-by-case examinations until all conceivable applications have had their bearing on the formulation of the maxim. Thus, in broad strokes, formalistic reasoning proceeds in a cyclical, reiterative manner from maxims to cases to principles and back to cases until all that bears upon formulation of the maxim for action is considered and a consensus is achieved. The array of cases discussed in this chapter points to the complexity and extent of such a process.

Philosophical Roots

The preceding view of formalistic reasoning is not wholly original. It has philosophical roots in several twentieth-century authors. One is John Rawls. His notion of *reflective equilibrium* has been described as a balancing of moral intuitions with one's principles for action.[23]

This proposal is also similar to Lyons's *method of rebuttals*.

Lyons describes it as successive modifications of principles based on examples and counterexamples and explains its cyclical nature in this way:

> The method of rebuttals is . . . based upon the fact that sometimes when we apply a particular moral principle in practice we are unable to take all relevant factors into account. And our failure to consider some factors results in our incorrectly inferring a judgement for or against an act from the principle. Thus, we want in practice to regard the judgements that we think are implied by the principle as tentative, subject to correction in case something significant proves to have been overlooked.[24]

Lyons's method implies that generalizing or universalizing in ethics is not an esoteric faculty but a historical succession of refinements to rules made possible by the examination of relevant cases.

In describing the process of scientific discovery, Alfred North Whitehead made a similar statement:

> The true method of discovery is like the flight of an aeroplane. It starts from the ground of particular observation; it makes a flight in the thin air of imaginative generalization; and it again lands for renewed observation rendered acute by rational interpretation.[25]

The essence of ethical formalism, as described in this book, is not unlike formal reasoning processes in philosophy and science generally. It involves discovery and change; but change in ethics does not imply relativism any more than change in science implies anything other than progress. The chief proof of the soundness of each is achievement. Therefore, although ethical formalism may fall short at any given moment in identifying absolute principles, its aim is to get us there as quickly as possible without claiming ethical knowledge prematurely or exploiting our perhaps naive respect for philosophical inquiry.

Kantian ethical analysis is not as abstract and cryptic as

most modern business-society authors suggest. Like utilitarianism, its chief purpose is to make our ideas clear enough so that we can act on them. Utilitarianism does this from the perspective of human feelings by thinking through the range of consequences of alternative actions and quantifying their worth according to the satisfaction of individuals' wants. It requires us to be clear about our preferences. Formalism, by contrast, is a more cognitive process and demands clarity of behavioral principles.

The similarity of practical formalism to legal reasoning raises the issue of the conflation of the distinction between moral and legal matters. But one must remember that the distinction is largely convergent; that is, the distinction between morality and the law applies to a comparatively small set of behaviors, which can be accounted for in terms of the shortcomings of the method in the social context. Furthermore, similarity of method does not imply similarity of subject: The scientific method, for example, is employed in a number of disciplines, and yet we do not reduce one discipline to another. So, the similarity of the method of practical formalism to legal reasoning does not constitute a weakness; on the contrary, it promotes respect for the law by pointing to its foundations in ethical reasoning.

The view of Kantian formalism presented in this book accomplishes several tasks. First, it shows us more clearly what utilitarianism is *not* designed to do. The division of labor in management ethics is complementary and productive: Utilitarians resolve questions of *degree*, and formalists resolve questions of *kind*.[26]

Second, the view presented in this chapter helps us to understand why formalism is said to focus on the "form" of an act. Contrary to what some authors argue, it is not related to the distinction between form and content, but rather to the contrast between *formal* and *casual*.[27] Formalistic analysis is highly concerned with the particular content of an act; but in contrast with casual actions, whose grounds lie in impulse and personal preference, formal ethical behavior is deliberate, reasoned, and considered.

Finally, this view of Kantian formalism preserves the relevance of philosophical discourse for business ethics. At a time when we are accused of "teaching ethics without ethics to teach"[28] and of promoting "ethical chic,"[29] a more practical understanding of Kantian formalism may boost the credibility of business ethics and promote a closer connection between improved managerial insight and rigorous philosophical analysis.

Summary of Key Concepts

1. As we learned in Chapter Three, Kantian ethics requires the universalizability of moral actions. This chapter explains what this requirement means.

2. At the heart of this method is a small set of *core values*, goals, or ideals, that serve together as necessary requirements for deliberation and action.

3. The relevance and application of these core values are worked out in our lives via seven forms of deliberation: extreme cases, counterfactual cases, analogies and metaphors, reverse cases, precedent, counterexamples, and archetypal cases.

4. The collection and comprehensive consideration of these kinds of cases allow us to organize our analysis of an issue by drawing distinctions and making generalizations.

5. Kant's requirement of universalizability is satisfied, then, in this way: An action that survives the scrutiny of all conceivable cases (described previously) is moral.

6. From a practical point of view, ethical formalism requires imagination and patience.

7. The method described in this chapter is not wholly original. It is similar to other descriptions of decision making by Rawls, Lyons, and Whitehead.

Questions and Exercises

1. Articulate the differences between the pairs of concepts in the "Distinctions" subsection of this chapter.

2. Arguments by analogy are sometimes more convincing than arguments to the point because they appeal to shared intuitions and are refuted only by identifying ways in which the analogy differs significantly from the original situation. Consider the function and the strength of the following argument by analogy for reverse discrimination:

   When I was a kid, I took the bus to school. We had an informal rule that you boarded the bus in the order that you arrived at the bus stop. I suppose the rule was originally meant to keep big kids from bullying their way onto the bus first. Jimmy was a little boy who lived right next to the bus stop. It was very important to him that he be the first one on the bus. Each morning he'd get up very early and rush to dress and eat his breakfast so that he'd arrive before the rest of us. One day, after several years of this, some of us decided to change the rule. The new rule was that we would get on the bus in order of size, with the smallest kids getting on first. The bus had become crowded, and we thought the smallest kids most needed a seat. Jimmy was angry that he could no longer get a seat. He felt he had worked hard at learning how to be best in the old system and that the new rule was designed to cheat him out of his rightfully earned spot. He couldn't help it if he was now one of the bigger kids, he argued. Why should his size be used against him? I had a hard time taking Jimmy's arguments seriously. The new rule seemed to be what we needed for the time being. It didn't really hurt us big kids to stand during the ride to school. Besides, Jimmy had been sitting for a long time. (Charles Lawrence III, "The Bakke Case: Are Racial Quotas Defensible?" *The Saturday Review*, October 15, 1977, p. 16)

3. Probably the best examples of formalistic reasoning occur in legal argumentation. And some of the best examples in

the law involve the history of the development of the concept of equality, as constructed through decisions of the U.S. Supreme Court. Examine such cases as *Regents v. Bakke, Weinberger v. Wiesenfeld,* and *Brown v. the Board of Education* for the kinds of cases and principles outlined in this chapter.

4. On practically a daily basis, interesting formalistic issues are handled by the Internal Revenue Service and state and local tax agencies. They are asked continually to decide what are considered business expenses, nonprofit organizations, goods donated to charities, and so on. And their formalistic task seems unending. Put yourself in their shoes: Suppose that someone claimed an exemption on the taxation of his home and property on the grounds that it was a church. This person had obtained a mail order certification as a minister in an unorthodox church for $5 and held "services" on Monday nights, which consisted of listening to inspiring records and casual talk. Would you grant this person a tax exemption? Why or why not? Where do you draw the line?

5. Is there such a thing as an exceptionless rule, that is, a rule for which there exist no conceivable counterexamples? How are the rules of games, say of baseball, different from the rules of business?

6. Is the policy of the U.S. government consistent in its approach to drugs, alcohol, and tobacco? Can you think of any important distinctions that warrant inconsistency of treatment?

7. Should college athletes be paid? Why should the fact that a person is a student prevent him from selling his talents to someone who is willing to pay? Certainly, colleges make huge revenues from student athletes, who are precluded by current National College Athletic Association rules from accepting salaries for their skills. And the rules against marketing one's skills are difficult to enforce. Why not recognize that college athletes are big money-makers and pay them for it?

8. Many cities have laws against "ticket scalping," that is, selling tickets for a major event at an inflated price and at a

location near the event. The laws differ from city to city, but what is ethically wrong with scalping? Is scalping more like extortion, or does it merely reflect free market behaviors?

9. Consider the case of a secretary who loyally follows instructions to lie about the boss's presence when callers ask to speak to her. Under what conditions is this wrong? Allowable? Is this any different from responding "I'm fine" when people ask "How are you" when in fact you have a cold?

10. Is alcoholism an illness? Using the techniques discussed in this chapter, examine the strength of the claim that illness is a good analogy for understanding the nature of alcoholism. Can you think of any counterexamples? Any other analogies that might be better?

7

Rules for Making Exceptions to Rules

Ordinarily, one might expect rules to define the limits of managerial rationality: Where our rules stop, our ability to generalize, to distinguish, to categorize, to perceive, to understand, and to manage also stop. Where we do have insight, we make definitions, adopt rules, specify requirements, accept principles, post procedures, produce regulations, and together follow a collection of norms, customs, standards, policies, and laws. Evidence of our lack of understanding is the failure to express that understanding in terms of shared principles or rules. Therefore, it would seem that the sphere of understanding and manageability is coterminous with the sphere of rules.

Nevertheless, administrators are often required to produce rational decisions that are not guided by the accepted rules — to extend the bounds of rationality into new territory day by day. Few rules are exceptionless, but exceptions are not made without adequate reason, either — not unless the administrator is willing to appear capricious, cynical, untrustworthy, inconsistent, or impulsive. Such lack of regard for rules promotes ethical anarchy and destructive contests of power. However, failure to manage the rules by adopting a rigid, inflexible posture toward their implementation commits what Alfred North Whitehead calls "the fallacy of misplaced concreteness": Rules are reified by the administrator and granted excessive importance as constraints on discretionary power.[1]

The purpose of this chapter, then, is highly practical: We

need a clearer understanding of how successful administrators make exceptions to rules when those exceptions are justified. Somewhere in the realm of moral vision between wide-eyed, idiosyncratic behavior, on the one hand, and myopic dogmatism, on the other, is the moral testing ground of administrative judgment, which requires, in the language of Peters and Waterman, simultaneous "looseness and tightness" with respect to the matter of organizing human effort.[2] For moral reasons, we must know how to make exceptions to rules.

Origins in Management Theory

Management theorists are primarily acquainted with the management of rules through their studies of bureaucracies. Thompson's discussion of *bureaupathologies*, such as resistance to change and the ritualistic attachment to routines and procedures, implies that one common fault of administrators is their inability to manage bureaucratic processes in a flexible way.[3] Merton's earlier discussion of bureaucratic dysfunctions also draws attention to the varieties of rigidity and impersonality that are symptomatic of the failure in bureaucracies to manage systems of rules.[4]

Others have shown interest in the status of rules in the organization. Perrow, Simon, and Heiner argue convincingly that environmental complexity is the chief reason for the existence of rules. Perrow argues that an organization's response to complexity is often a reduction in the number of rules, that is, it mechanizes to reduce jobs, it standardizes personnel to reduce the variety of persons, it seals off the organization to buffer it from environmental complexity, and it reduces the number of products.[5] Simon's famous argument that administrators often seek satisfactory rather than optimal choices places human limits on the extension of rationality to decision making because of complexity.[6] And Heiner has recently argued, consistent with Simon, that refusing to make an exception, even under certain circumstances where that choice would probably enhance performance, can nevertheless be described as rational.[7]

So, the question of the place of rules in the organization

has received wide attention in the traditional management literature, but its relevance extends to more than bureaucratic dysfunctions. Deciding the grounds for making an exception to a rule is seen as a central topic in a variety of management issues: It is the substance of managerial discretion; it is the impetus for organizational change; it defines the boundaries of employee loyalty; it sets limits on the influence of the profit motive in business.

The focus of management theorists, however, has been on the psychological or sociological aspects of decision making as they relate to bureaucratic behaviors. This chapter argues that at least some bureaupathologies originate in the ethics of rule construction and, therefore, focuses on the *ethical* analysis of this issue, since it presents itself as the generic form of the problem of deciding when to make exceptions to rules. A fundamental problem for ethics is the criticism of rules. Like pieces of behavior, rules themselves may be judged to be more or less good or bad, thus requiring some technique for judging when to apply or not to apply a rule. What follows in this chapter, then, is an examination of the ethical grounds for making exceptions to rules. By attending to strictly rational and ethical grounds for rule management, judgment can be enhanced and both bureaupathologies and anarchic disregard for rules can be minimized.

Two Rules for Managing Rules

In seeking to discover these rational principles behind the making of *exceptions* to rules, we are also identifying the normative principles that guide the *construction* of rules. For if rules perfectly conformed to the normative requirements of their construction in the first place, there could never be rational grounds for later making exceptions to such rules. Therefore, the limits of rationality in managerial decision making lie in a set of ultimate normative principles, or *meta-rules*, to which all other behavior-guiding rules, policies, and regulations must conform. To the extent that our rules and regulations fall short of the normative requirements established by the set of meta-rules, exceptions to our rules can be identified that bring those rules more into conformance with the set of ultimate principles.

The source of the principles, or meta-rules, proposed in this chapter is related to the classical polarization in ethical theory developed in this book. We have referred to it as the confrontation between utilitarian and formalist (deontological) ethics.[8] By way of review, utilitarianism basically consists of the situational assessment of the comparative worth of acts, with the aim of producing the greatest overall good. To utilitarians, rules are useful only as summary generalizations of experience and can themselves be evaluated for their comparative worth. Formalists, by contrast, focus on the universality of practices and the possibility of developing absolute guidelines, or rules, for behavior. As we have seen in earlier chapters, the differences in these two positions are complex, and various hybrid views have also been developed; but for the purposes of this chapter, a simplified view of these positions is more useful. Expressed in simple terms, the confrontation of these two ethical theories reduces to the following question: How does one (1) take into account differential talents, abilities, wants, and needs to bring about as much good as possible for collections of individuals in a way that, at the same time, (2) recognizes their significant commonalities as expressed through mutual regard or the bond of membership? Even simpler: People are human beings by virtue of both their similarities and their differences; how does one justly recognize the significance of these diverging sets of features when trying to produce rules for behavior?[9]

These rather simple characterizations of utilitarian and formalist positions are relevant not just for understanding what happens in ethical decisions per se, but in accounting for the kinds of thinking that are done when *establishing* rules for behavior. The polarizing influence of the two ethical positions can be seen in even the most routine business decisions. Consider the common managerial problem of the allocation of resources. Suppose, for example, that a department has been allocated three new personal computers for its 15 employees. How are they to be assigned? Two sets of related options are possible:

Set A	*Set B*
1. Assign the computers to those whose skills allow them to make the best use of the new equipment.	1. Place the computers in a neutral location and allow open use on a first come, first served basis.
2. Allocate their use according to need.	2. Randomly rotate use of the computers by week, month, and so on.
3. Allocate the computers for personal or political reasons.	3. Develop a temporary centralized computer services office serving departmentwide needs.

There may be additional ways to resolve such an issue. The important illustration here lies in the *two perspectives* that generate the rules found in each set. Set *A* consists of utilitarian options that attempt to utilize the computers or maximize their value by allocating them in a discriminating way. These options *differentiate* among employees and appeal to unique or comparative differences among employees in order to justify discriminatory or selective allocation of the personal computers. Set *B* options, on the other hand, do not differentiate: instead, they promote the good by *identifying* employees as having common or equivalent claims to the computers. The various options listed in this set specify ways in which their treatment can be universalized and their commonality respected. Thus, the choices in set *B* reflect the influence of formalist interests.

Similarly, many common business practices or policies illustrate the effects of each of these two dominant ethical perspectives in generating rules for behavior:

1. *Differentiating (Utilitarian) Policies*
   a. Preference to hire graduates of particular universities
   b. Express lines at grocery stores
   c. Special VIP and press seating at the ballpark
   d. Cash discounts
   e. Year-end merit bonuses
   f. No change made for noncustomers

     g. Customer parking only

     h. Minimum order amounts; discounts for large orders

2. *Identifying (Formalistic) Policies*

     a. No cash refunds

     b. Per-customer limits on merchandise

     c. Some traffic laws (four-way stops, etc.)

     d. Open seating at the theater

     e. Salary schedules (as opposed to negotiated salaries)

     f. Dress codes (to bring about identification with the organization)

     g. Deadlines

     h. Uniforms

Such sets of policies, or rules, illustrate the polarizing and often independent influence that the differentiating and identifying factors have in rule construction.

The influence of these two ethical positions extends from the level of personal decisions to the organization of societies. Ideologically, social Darwinism, for example, clearly emphasizes the differences among human beings, while a philosophy like Marxism focuses on their similarities. Even sectors of society differ with respect to how these two principles are employed. The worlds of athletics and business, of course, are dominated by the need to differentiate, while government, religion, and the family tend to identify persons' positions and to attribute ethically equivalent (or even joint) status. Government policymakers are often caught in the middle of these counterpoised principles, needing to devise policies that balance the interests of, say, families and businesses; Okun's account of the trade-off between equality and efficiency in designing public policy illustrates the point.[10] Therefore, the differentiation-identification dichotomy lies at the root of rule formation throughout the entire range of personal and social organization.

In the sections that follow, these insights into ethical theory and the polar generation of normative behavior are translated into a more practical form and are presented as two meta-rules for the construction of normative rules. Thus, to the degree that our administrative rules fail to conform to these meta-rules, the meta-rules themselves become the grounds for exceptions to our rules and policies. The differentiating principle is named the *principle of benefaction*; the identifying principle is named the *principle of membership*.

The Principle of Benefaction

The first principle is the principle of benefaction. To theoreticians in the utilitarian tradition, it is referred to as *maximizing utility*; but, because of its abstraction, this traditional title fails to call attention to the *administrative factor* beyond the system of organizational rules. Presumably, the reason we have administrators in addition to systems of rules is because such systems are organic and require management, and because good management can produce an increment of value beyond that which could be obtained by mechanical enforcement of the rules. Good administrators, therefore, are *benefactors* in rule management.

The principle of benefaction, in its most general application, simply admonishes policymakers to discriminate among individuals' situations and then to design, adjust, and administer rules in order to promote the most good or satisfaction among that population of individuals. But because few if any rules or policies anticipate all eventualities, the principle of benefaction can be simplified and restated to make clear its relevance for this chapter: "Make an exception to a rule when greater overall good or satisfaction will occur by so doing." Consider the following case.

A harried business executive, Victor Timm, received a phone call from his wife, asking him to drop by the city zoo on the way home from work and pick up a ceramic mug from the gift shop just inside the zoo's front gates. Being a regular annual contributor to "Friends of the Zoo," and having also arranged for modest corporate support, Mr. Timm did not mind visiting one of his more favorite locations.

On arriving, however, he found that the zoo had just closed, displaying the following sign: "Entrance gates close at 4 P.M.; all patrons must leave by 6 P.M." At first feeling rather frustrated, he then reasoned, "The 4 P.M. closing

141

time is a good policy, assuming that all who pay to visit the zoo will wish to stay for at least two hours to get their money's worth. But I am a Zoological Society member and have a pass that admits me free of charge for a year. Furthermore, I only wish to visit the gift shop to purchase a $5 ceramic mug." Appealing to a security guard and to other entrance personnel had no effect. "What are rules for if you ask us to break them?" they replied. Turned away at the gate, Victor Timm simply could not understand what overriding inconvenience to the zoo personnel could be greater than his own by forcing him to return another day. Two letters asking for an explanation from the general manager of the zoo finally elicited only a brief response: "It would be impossible to accommodate the great number of people requesting considerations that are not in line with our policies."

Those who have felt victimized by such bureaucratic administrators, who allow themselves to become managed by the rules they themselves have created, can sympathize with the frustrated businessman in this case. The failure of the general manager to delegate discretionary power to entrance personnel consists in failing to provide rational insight into the contextual function of the policy. Although a split-time closing policy is clearly better than a single closing time, since it avoids the need to make exceptions for patrons who pay for admission shortly before closing, the split-time policy creates its own (if smaller) class of exceptions. Pass-holding patrons are needlessly constrained by the policy. The general manager's response illustrates a typically bureaucratic inability to appreciate an exception to a rule when it involves little or no cost to the organization.

The principle of benefaction reminds the administrator that the application or enforcement of a rule depends on the circumstances. The following is a set of exceptions to rules that are justified by the principle of benefaction:

1. *John Rawls's Difference Principle.* Rawls argues that, as a general rule, all members of society should benefit

equally from available resources. The one significant exception to this rule is a principle he calls the *difference principle*, which states: "socio-economic differences are to be arranged so that they are . . . reasonably expected to be to everyone's advantage."[11] This principle allows for the recognition and promotion of individual abilities so long as the exercise of those abilities results in benefit to the entire group, especially those who are most disadvantaged. Applying this principle, for example, we might allow some persons to become exceptionally wealthy if, in the process, they performed services vital to the rest of society.

2. ***Special Provisions for Skilled Personnel.*** Even though standard working hours may apply across the organization generally, non-standard hours may be arranged by exception for certain employees, such as computer programmers or maintenance personnel.

3. ***Incomplete Differentiating Formulas.*** Judgments regarding admission to special training programs are often expressed in terms of a formulaic relation among test scores or other quantitative variables. When such a formula fails to assess all the relevant variables (such as a supervisor's strong recommendation), exceptions may be made on the grounds of the principle of benefaction.

The principle of benefaction is not without significant constraints and shortcomings. It assumes that a manager's ability to maximize utility in enforcing rules is limited by all the standard shortcomings of utilitarian analysis.[12] This includes the problem of the deep ambiguity of the word *utility* as it relates to judging comparative utility. So, although there is considerable looseness in explicating the principle of benefaction, in general the application of this principle is warranted to the degree that the overall good is enhanced.

The Principle of Membership

Because the principle of benefaction is closely tied to the utilitarian tradition, one might expect it to be vulnerable at similar points. Perhaps the chief weakness in utilitarian thinking is the problem of justice.[13] As we saw in Chapter Three, in some cases maximally good results can be achieved only by treating some individuals or groups unfairly. But this criticism is not based on the principle of benefaction; it is made in spite of it. The unfairness judged to hold in cases of maldistributed resources is brought to light by the application of a second management principle, the principle of membership.

The principle of membership guides rule construction by focusing on persons' *similarities*, not their differences. In terms of Kantian ethical theory, it represents the requirement that our actions and the rules prescribing those actions be universalizable and that in this respect all persons are equal citizens in a "kingdom of ends." In contrast to the principle of benefaction, which exhibits *partialities* for reasons of *utility*, the principle of membership implies *impartiality* for reasons of *affiliation*. This principle, therefore, is similar to the principle of equality, except that from the administrator's point of view it calls attention to the *grounds* of equality, which lie in being a member of a certain class. (Think of the long history of the extension of human rights in the United States, in which the degree of similarity among classes of persons has been the crucial issue.)

The principle of membership, expressed from the practical point of view of most managers, requires the recognition and honoring of commonalities among the persons under one's supervision. Managers are more than loci of utility production; they are also stewards of the common bond among persons. This bond may reside in their membership in the human race, their national citizenship, their organizational affiliation, or other associations that are often expressed in terms of mutual rights and obligations.

Stated as simply as possible, the principle of membership requires exceptions to rules when doing so recognizes or promotes the affiliation and connectedness of persons; it challenges the administrator to account for why anyone under his or her supervision should be treated any differently from anyone else. Examples of its use to make exceptions include the following:

1. *Group-wide Distributions.* Giving tickets to a local professional sporting contest to all the employees of the firm may be an exception to the usual practice of distributing them selectively on the basis of performance.

2. *Excessive Discrimination.* For example, hiring a woman or a minority member might be an exception to a traditional practice of discriminative hiring.

3. *Employee Rights.* Recognition of employee rights is an exception to a more general notion of the property rights of employers. Such rights stand counterposed to a variety of differentiating processes that, in the extreme, might exploit vulnerable persons. A fair wage can be claimed by employees who otherwise may be exploited or abused. This, of course, is most true where the claim of membership is strongest: It is easier for citizens to demand a fair wage than for aliens.

4. *Constitutionality.* The Constitution is often applied to make exceptions in cases where differentiating policies might otherwise ignore one's citizenship or membership in a community. Union contracts are also notorious for emphasizing affiliational concerns over individual differences; their successes can be regarded as exceptions to the general rule of securing and rewarding individual productivity.

5. *Excessive or Arbitrary Differentiation.* A common organizational problem is excessive differentiation, which often occurs because of organizational policies or rules. Managers may wish to reward or recognize individuals or groups for meritorious performance; but where this may be perceived to be arbitrary, excessive, disruptive, or alienating, the principle of membership may warrant interrupting or restraining the practice.

6. *Special Provisions for the Handicapped.* Organizations often go to great lengths to provide the handicapped with full membership and equal opportunity.

The precise meaning of *membership* (or *equality* or *equity*) is dependent upon the nature of the group in which membership is claimed. The principle of membership means different things for families, clubs, religions, businesses, teams, and nations in terms of the distribution of burdens and benefits. Even in the business world, employee membership is recognized less in small businesses than in large ones, where ownership rights are diffuse and employee rights begin to assert themselves in terms of various protections and privileges. Therefore, there is no invariant definition of the principle of membership, just as there is considerable looseness in the definition of the principle of benefaction. Although these principles are highly abstract and elude mechanical explication of their requirements, practical examples of their use are easy to find, as the next section shows.

Practical Implications

Good managing requires the skillful application of the two principles discussed previously in the context of organizational life. Large variances in organizational climate can be established using these principles. The manager can promote the unity of team spirit or cooperation by applying the principle of membership or can emphasize the principle of benefaction by differentiating among employees and promoting controlled competition, implementing a hierarchy of control, merit bonuses, and so on. Under what conditions this occurs, and how each principle is to be applied, is the focus of this section.

One way of beginning to understand the interrelation of the two principles discussed previously is to examine their *misapplication*. The generality of the principles discourages a tight mechanical display of their application, but an examination of their violation testifies to their relevance in cases where the principles can be evoked to rectify the problem.

Balancing the Two Principles

Either principle, when employed exclusively or allowed to dominate the other, leads to abuse in the construction and enforcement of rules. The principle of benefaction is misapplied, for example, when the administrator becomes too impressed with the differences among employees, allowing competition to become destructive and individuality to dominate sociality. The overuse of the principle of benefaction sacrifices affiliations and relationships, sometimes resulting in exploitation. Both free riders and sacrificial lambs can, under certain circumstances, be justified according to the principle of benefaction, but they violate the principle of membership and lead to forms of fragmentation and alienation best described by Marx.

The principle of membership is abused when managers become too impressed with equality, group identity, conserving membership, and other bureaupathologies.[14] This abuse is illustrated by impersonality, a predisposition against idiosyncracy, and the fear of contamination. Perrow refers to this as *purging particularism* from bureaucracies.[15] In attending to group identity, the abuse sacrifices innovation, cooperation of differential elements of the group, and suppresses individual talents and desires. Such tendencies are common in bureaucracies, where membership and collective action often dominate individual discriminations. Perrow attributes such administrative behavior to personal insecurity. Thus, the exclusive use of either principle results in its own form of wastefulness, unfairness, and narrow-mindedness.

By contrast, giving due regard to the claims of both principles prevents dominant attention from being given to either principle, and managers should strive to achieve this tension in their management of organizational rules. Examples of where a balance of the two principles is achieved include the following:

1. The athletic coach who has had to balance team unity with performance in making room for an eccentric but valuable player knows this well.

2. The National and American League All-Star Baseball teams are chosen using a balanced approach that illustrates the two principles: All the starting players, except pitchers, are chosen by fan ballot (the principle of benefaction), and each league team must have at least one representative, protecting good players in fran-

147

chises that are not "media capitals" (the principle of membership).

3. Neighbors also experience this delicate balance when they become aware that although they are free not to mow their lawns, for example, the quality of the neighborhood is a function of general cooperation in such matters.

4. Tax laws attempt to balance the ability to pay with paying one's share.

5. Traffic systems have some laws that recognize priorities (the general right-of-way of freeway traffic) and others that treat individuals alike (four-way stops).

Elster describes this ideal situation as *control without rigidity*,[16] Peters and Waterman as a simultaneous *looseness and tightness* of principles,[17] and Pascale and Athos as *balancing*.[18]

So, although judging the respective contributions of each of the principles from case to case may be a rather subjective project, the balanced influence of both principles in the overall context of administration seems clear. This is reflected in the Latin phrase that adorns our coins: *E pluribus unum* ("Unity in diversity"). It is also echoed in various lines from "America, the Beautiful": "Crown thy good with brotherhood" and "Confirm thy soul in self control, thy liberty in law."

Rule Design and Enforcement Issues

Even when rules are well formulated, exceptions can be made for the kinds of reasons previously mentioned. However, rules are not always well formulated, and the following discussion explores some typical administrative failings to conform to the meta-rules outlined earlier.

1. *Administering the Principle of Benefaction.* One of the problems in applying the principle of benefaction consists in the fact that rules themselves seldom distinguish between behaviors as examples of social patterns and behaviors as idiosyncratic events. Some behaviors, for example, are beneficial or harmful at a certain

threshold level of repeated occurrence but would be inconsequential regarded individually.[19] In this general case, the principle of benefaction would be violated, for example, if traffic officers gave parking tickets to cars in lots that were virtually empty. That is, the purpose of providing parking spaces for those with permits is hardly served by issuing tickets at times when there is low demand for the spaces, but would be more appropriate as spaces for permit holders became increasingly difficult to find.

The principle of benefaction is also difficult to administer when there may be confusion over the significance of the differences appealed to. When applying the principle of benefaction, differences are appealed to that may be either weak or strong, real or illusory. The success of much advertising, for example, turns on the ability to convince consumers of the significance of product differences that may be only cosmetic; thus, the rational consumer searches for real differences in applying the principle of benefaction. The rational administrator, similarly, must be certain that the indicators of performance are real, lest hirings and promotions be made for inadequate reasons, such as strengths that apply only to a previous job.

2. *Administering the Principle of Membership.* Often it is administratively impossible to formulate a rule so that it refers precisely to the class of persons intended. For example, a rule disallowing beverage containers in the ballpark may be intended to produce greater sobriety among the fans, but it also inadvertently affects those who might have brought nonalcoholic beverages of their own to the park. The earlier case involving the zoo also illustrates the mismatch of rule and circumstance in that the rule was intended to prevent only paying customers from being frustrated by getting less than full value for their money; pass holders need not have been affected. In such circumstances, exceptions can be justified to tailor the policy to the demands of the principle of membership.

Another historical example of poor principle formulation involves the popular game of bowling. Brought to the United States in the 1600s by the Dutch, and originally known as *nine-pins*, the game added a tenth pin in response to a law in New York that specifically outlawed the game of nine-pins because it was associated with heavy gambling. Not forbidding bowling in general, the law was circumvented by the addition of a tenth pin.

The principle of membership requires also that rules be formulated that capture real and substantial affinities among alleged members of a group. The failure to do so might be illustrated by attempts to unionize professionals, whose affinities are much weaker than those of, say, blue-collar workers. A second example comes from Melville Dalton, who found that membership in the Masonic Order was virtually a prerequisite to managerial advancement.[20]

A Template for Rule Management

In order to promote the *rational* approach to rule management and to simplify the kinds of insights that make bureaupathological and entrepreneurial anarchic behavior more difficult to defend, the following *template for rule management* is provided. It collects and presents the major points of this discussion in a simplified format. Using this template, employees charged with the responsibility of enforcing new policies should review the implications of those policies in order to promote appreciation of the function of rules, enhance good judgment, and facilitate the delegation of discretionary power.

The making of exceptions to rules is more of an aesthetic skill than an exercise of mechanical efficiency. The word *exception* is just a linguistic marker for a loose cluster of situations that are circumscribed by the meta-rules discussed in this chapter. I've tried to demonstrate here that all systems of rules conform simultaneously to the demands of two general principles and that capable managers sense these principles, even if they do not always express them. This chapter has attempted to articulate these antipodal demands. And while their explication may be abstract and difficult, the template provided for

		The Principle of Benefaction	*The Principle of Membership*
1.	Dominant setting	Entrepreneurial Small business Competitive	Bureaucratic Large organizations Cooperative
2.	Dysfunctions	Excessive competition Excessive individualism Alienation	Lethargy Deindividuation Fear of intrusion
3.	Grounds for application	High benefit Low cost	Restrain free riders Prevent sacrificial lambs
4.	Administrative requirements	Threshold or linear utility? Are the differences a. real? b. reasonable? c. compatible?	Accurate reference to the group? Are the affinities a. real? b. substantial? c. worthy?

Template for Rule Management

the examination of rules and policies is designed to promote application of these principles to particular cases — increasing the influence of the rational while subduing the merely personal or political aspects of rule management. Thus, the typical bureaucratic dysfunctions described by Thompson, Merton, and others, as well as forms of anarchic or entrepreneurial exploitation, may be more easily avoided through heightened rational awareness of the interplay and function of rules.

Explicating how managers make exceptions to rules also makes us more aware of the irreducible conceptual, or even philosophical, component of managerial decision making. The successful managing of systems of rules requires a full range of thinking — from the very concrete to the very abstract, from the mundane to the philosophical. And the ability to make even minor exceptions when called for reflects a competence in merging the disparate elements underlying this process into an accepted judgment.

However, one must not assume that managerial decisiveness is the exclusive goal of this chapter. The achievement of value in human life is a *process* to be experienced that can sometimes be ignored or circumvented by managing that is too efficient. Where the journey is as important as the end result, managerial efficiency is not necessarily desirable. Therefore, administrative restraint sometimes requires alternative acts to decision making out of respect for democratic processes and the fullness of human relationships and experiences.[21] Being "decisive" is sometimes just a euphemism for simple-mindedness or administrative arrogance, while apparent administrative lethargy is not always pathological.

Summary of Key Concepts

1. There are three kinds of administrators; two are bad. One never makes exceptions to rules; another has little regard for rules and makes exceptions for a variety of reasons. But the third type makes exceptions only when appropriate. The purpose of this chapter is to understand better the third type of administrator.

2. "Rigid, inflexible bureaucrat" is a common stereotype, and various theorists have examined this phenomenon. The true nature of rules in organizations is a long-standing theoretical problem.

3. Utilitarianism and formalism each assert their own requirements regarding how rules are formulated and enforced. Utilitarianism requires that rules take into account important differences among people and so arrange things that the results will be good; formalism requires that rules attend to the similarities among people and so arrange things that the sense of membership, belonging, or equality is preserved. In other words, rules in organizations serve both to differentiate and to identify components of the organization.

4. Two principles for the construction of rules are derived from the influence of the utilitarian and formalistic requirements discussed. They are the principles of benefaction and membership. When some existing organizational rule or policy falls short in a particular situation in satisfying either principle, that principle can be appealed to as grounds for an exception to the rule.

5. Rules are designed best when the influence of these two principles is balanced. Failing to do so, and allowing either principle to dominate in an organization, results in anarchy or rigid bureaucracy, respectively.

6. Some rules have threshold levels of useful application such that enforcing the rule makes no utilitarian sense when violations are either rare or rampant. Only when

the growing number of violations threatens to change the general practice of conformance is enforcing the rule appropriate.

7. Rules must also be designed so that they refer only to the class of persons or the behavior intended. The failure to do so creates loopholes and the possibility of unanticipated technical exceptions.

Questions and Exercises

1. Make a list of rules from the organization in which you work. For each, state whether its primary function is to differentiate, is to identify, or seems to balance the two interests.

2. Sometimes customary behavior conflicts with the rule book. It's difficult to know what to do in those circumstances. Which rule should be followed—custom or the official rule?

   In the history of sports, one of the best examples of this conflict of rules occurred on September 23, 1908, at the Polo Grounds in New York, where the Giants and the Cubs were tied 1–1 in the bottom of the ninth inning. The Giants were up; they had runners at first (Merkle) and third (McCormick) bases, with two men out. The batter then hit a clean single to deep right center field.

   Today that would end the game. The runner on third raced home for the winning run, and apparently the game was over. However, as Merkle headed for second and saw that the winning run had crossed the plate, he turned and ran for the clubhouse—customary behavior in that situation in 1908. Then the second baseman, Johnny Evers, got a ball, stepped on second base, and appealed to the umpires for a game-ending force play. The umpires disagreed for several hours. Later that evening, Merkle was ruled out at second, the run did not count, and a game the Giants had thought they had won was ruled a tie.

   A week later when the regular season ended, these same two teams—the Giants and the Cubs—were tied for first place. Therefore, the tie game from a week earlier had to be replayed to decide who would go to the World Series. The Cubs won, and from then on Merkle was called "Bonehead."

   a. Can you think of any other examples where customary behavior ("Everybody does it") conflicts with an official but seldom enforced rule?

   b. Some might say that the Giants–Cubs game was decided on a technicality. How important are technicalities in sports? In business?

     c. What is the relationship between a society's laws and its customary behavior? Does one come before the other? Do laws serve a purpose even when they cannot be enforced?

3. Ursula LeGuin's book *The Dispossessed* is a science fiction novel that portrays two civilizations: Annares, a resource-scarce society that allows no personal property, and A-Io, a prosperous society founded on the idea of property. Which society best reflects the application of the principle of membership? The principle of benefaction? Do you think LeGuin would argue for the moral superiority of either?

4. The legislature of the United States is a balance of the Senate and the House of Representatives. Which reflects the principles of utilitarian organization? Of formalistic organization?

5. What exceptions would you be willing to make to the following general rules, and why?
   a. Always tell the truth.
   b. Never kill.
   c. No shirt, no shoes, no service.
   d. No students will be late for the exam.
   e. Don't come to work if you have the flu.
   f. All employees must wear uniforms.
   g. Checks will not be cashed without two forms of identification.
   h. Employees who are habitually late will be reprimanded.
   i. No smoking.

6. One of the practical problems associated with the management of rules or policies in organizations is the difficulty of expecting employees to conform to the rules without knowing much about the reason for them. People are more likely to obey the rules when they understand the reason or purpose behind the rules.

   The following is a rule on a sign found at the entrance to the Wimbledon Tennis Tournament. Do you think it is possible to make our organizational rules look more like this? (The underlined portion is what we are accustomed to seeing.)

> Flash photography is forbidden, as it is most off-putting to players and public alike and in any case will have no effect at such distance from the court.

7. The two main principles discussed in the chapter, benefaction and membership, provide some of the reasons for our purchases. For example, department store salespersons often coax us to buy a product because it is their "most popular item" or because "there's not another one like it." How do these appeals to one's ego illustrate the two principles of this chapter?

8. In his book *Equality and Efficiency: The Big Tradeoff*, Arthur Okun ends with the following words: "Capitalism and democracy are a most improbable mixture. Maybe that is why they need each other—to put some rationality into equality and some humanity into efficiency" (p. 120). How does his statement relate to the main themes of this chapter?

9. Suppose one of your best friends approaches you with the following proposal: "Look, I know a sure-fire way to make some big bucks this year. But we each have to put up some money up front. Here's the plan: You go in for ten thousand dollars and I'll do the same. We rent a small building about a block away from the grammar school and furnish it with video game equipment. I've seen it done in other places; the kids love it. I'm sure we can walk away from the deal at the end of the year splitting a hundred thousand dollars!" What do you do? How does this issue call upon the principle of benefaction?

10. Should campuses have honors programs for the best students? This would involve giving those students special privileges, such as advance registration, dormitory priority, parking privileges, and so on. Does it make any difference if the campus is crowded and resources are already stretched thin? How do the principles of benefaction and membership interact in this problem?

11. Many health and exercise clubs have limits on the use of certain popular equipment, such as exercise bicycles. A common policy might be to limit any person's use of such equipment to no more than 25 minutes at a time. What principles are operating here? Should these limited-use policies be enforced when very few persons are around? Should they be enforced when the equipment is in such demand that the facility couldn't give even 5 minutes of use to all those who want it?

12. One of the clearest illustrations of the tension between the principles of benefaction and membership is in *lifeboat ethics* situations. Several such experiential games are well known in the field of management, and they always begin with a critical resource that cannot be made available to the present group, forcing some decisions to be made about "who is in" and "who is out." A typical game might provide brief descriptions of a dozen employees in an imaginary firm that is faced with mandatory layoffs and then require the participants in the game to decide which six (say) employees will be laid off. Some of the reasons given for such decisions are listed. Which reflect the principle of benefaction? Of membership?
    a. He is young; being laid off here won't hurt him too much.
    b. She is a single parent; it might be harder for her to find work.
    c. So-and-so has been with the firm for 25 years; he deserves to be retained.
    d. She is our most productive worker; keep her.
    e. Let's have a lottery; the first six drawn are laid off.
    f. "Last in, first out."
    g. He's a member of a disadvantaged minority; keep him.

8

Ethical Theory and Art

The foregoing chapters imply that ethical justification is nothing more than the product of good, clear thinking. But ethical *behavior* is more than this. As with any other human activity, the ability to perform usually outstrips the ability to articulate, explain, or teach that performance to another. In other words, there are standards of performance in ethics that are difficult to capture in terms of the analytic categories described in the previous chapters of this book. Nevertheless, they are compatible with those categories. But just as one can be a good art critic without being a good artist, one can think clearly in ethics without necessarily being ethically competent. The purpose of this chapter is to investigate how one goes beyond good thinking in ethics to "good doing."

A major theme of this project is the claim that ethical behavior is truly aesthetic; good persons are beautiful persons. Glancing at the titles of some recent books on management, one might get the impression that theorists are taking seriously the proposition that managing is an art form. One finds books on the "art" of being a boss, being an executive, Japanese management, managing managers, playing safe on Wall Street, and so on. The titles are more faddish than serious. With even less development and application than ethical theory, the assertions connecting managing and art turn out to be hollow. For a reader interested in aesthetics, a book on the

159

joy of managing would sell more copies and disappoint only slightly less.

The attention of this chapter, therefore, is somewhat bifocal: It aims to understand better the relation of utilitarianism and formalism in ethical theory, and it attempts to account for the not well understood appeal of aesthetic categories in business literature. It does so, first, by distinguishing between two ways of knowing and by taking some of the mystery out of claims to intuitive business insight. This distinction also helps to account for the impotence of ethical theory, as well as for the currently popular idea that there is something artful about managing well.

Two Forms of Knowing

The object of ethical inquiry is knowledge, just as it is in sociology, chemistry, or meteorology. These disciplines also display procedures of discovery that warrant the claim to knowledge, such as statistical, laboratory, or experimental techniques. Ethical theory, too, has traditionally sought a decision procedure that would bestow credibility on its claims to moral knowledge, and the foregoing chapters represent an attempt to come to terms in a practical way with these procedures in ethics.

Where justification or explanation in ethics is concerned, these studies are all important and illustrate a form of awareness (or knowing) that is assumed in most academic studies. But ethics, especially ethical behavior, is not wholly accounted for in terms of one mode of awareness only; part of the focus of ethical inquiry is a second form of knowing that may be more difficult to explicate but is just as important as the first. The distinction between these two ways of knowing is reasonably well known but less well appreciated, and it provides insight into the frustration and confusion that one sometimes confronts in trying to link ethical theory to business issues.

Gilbert Ryle first called attention to two ways of knowing in *The Concept of Mind*.[1] The distinction, put very simply, consists of the difference between *knowing how* and *knowing that*. Think of this distinction in terms of what the typical business executive can be expected to know:

Know that:	*Know how:*
interest rates influence business growth	to inspire subordinates
employees are more produc- tive where goals are clear and realistic	to make an exception to a rule
	to write concise reports

These two forms of knowledge can be differentiated in various ways, but one important feature is the susceptibility to verbal articulation. The general incompatibility between knowing how and verbal articulation is illustrated by Ryle in discussing boxing skill:

> Whether or not the boxer plans his maneuvers before executing them, his cleverness at boxing is decided in the light of how he fights. If he is a Hamlet of the ring, he will be condemned as an inferior fighter, though perhaps a brilliant theorist or critic. Cleverness at fighting is exhibited in the giving and parrying of blows, not in the acceptance or rejection of propositions about blows. . . .[2]

That is, when in the act of exhibiting a knowing how, step-by-step descriptions or analyses only obstruct the processes important to that form of knowing. This does not mean that a skilled boxer could not also be a boxing analyst, critic, or teacher; indeed, some ability is required for such insight. As Ryle adds,

> For one person to see the jokes that another makes, the one thing he must have is a sense of humor and even that special brand of sense of humor of which those jokes are exercises.[3]

Nevertheless, it is important to see that the forms of knowing required by performing, on the one hand, and by analysis and understanding, on the other, are different.

Similarly, in his book *The Tacit Dimension*, Michael Polanyi argues that "we can know more than we can tell."[4] Among the vast array of human skills that appear to transcend complete verbal description are these:

1. Diagnosing diseases successfully
2. Riding a bicycle
3. Tasting wines or teas
4. Determining the sex of baby chicks

Perhaps this distinction helps to account for the attention given in business circles to *mentors*. A relationship with a mentor is typically more personal than with a teacher, as some managerial skills are acquired by firsthand experience and emulation and not by mere conceptualization. Less is said and more is done. The mastering of many business skills may be subtle — even artistic — by comparison with the verbal transfer of information and knowledge, but it is not without its own structure and patterns of learning. Polanyi refers to these kinds of abilities as a *tacit dimension* of human knowledge, a dimension where normally such knowledge is not adequately articulated. Such knowledge is not acquired by precept or verbal instruction so much as by example, practice, and repetition.

Polanyi's *tacit dimension* roughly corresponds to Ryle's *knowing how*, and Polanyi's implied *verbal dimension* matches the domain of *knowing that*. Consequently, because language is essentially a shared ability, theoretical or factual knowledge must be public, while knowing how is less closely linked to language and is therefore more personal.[5]

This distinction is also reflected in the writings of various other philosophers. Hans Reichenbach differentiates, for example, between (1) the *context of discovery*, which is creative and escapes logical analysis, and (2) the *context of justification*, which is a logical account of observation and experience.[6] Similarly, Jean-Paul Sartre distinguishes between the *positional* (objective) consciousness and the *nonpositional* (self-aware) consciousness.[7] Thus, the general distinction between two forms of knowledge is well known to philosophers.

Although the distinction is conceptually sturdy, it is not linguistically clean. Some managerial skills, such as knowing how to work with computers, strongly lend themselves to textbook and other forms of verbal instruction. Similarly, we speak of some business decisions as though they are more closely connected to talents born from experience than from books, such as knowing that "now is the time to buy," "Patterson is the right person for the job," or "the company will profit from advertising its top-of-the-line product most heavily." So, although knowing how and knowing that are fairly transparent distinctions, in daily language the two forms of knowing are closely linked. Indeed, as Polanyi suggests, "These two aspects of knowing have a similar structure and neither is ever present without the other."[8]

Recent neurophysiological research also supports the general psychological distinction between knowing how and knowing that. Although speculation regarding the implication of research in hemispheric laterality has resulted in an avalanche of popular literature in recent years (causing more cautious researchers to complain of the "dichotomania" exhibited by excessively optimistic or speculative theorists), recent research does point to a general distinction between elemental and contextual processing that is related to asymmetrical processes in the two cerebral hemispheres. Springer and Deutsch conclude, for example:

> The sequential–simultaneous distinction reflects a current, though not universally accepted, theoretical model holding that the left hemisphere tends to deal with rapid changes in time and to analyze stimuli in terms of details and features, while the right hemisphere deals with simultaneous relationships and with the more global properties of patterns.[9]

This neurophysiological research appears to coincide nicely with the conceptual distinctions made by Ryle, Polanyi, and others. Knowing how is generally a very complex skill that demands contextual or simultaneous mental processing probably related to the right hemisphere; the left hemisphere is more involved with the successive processing of discrete elements, lending itself more to verbal forms of knowing, or knowing that. The distinction between these two forms of knowledge is important, I think, for obtaining insight into various aspects of managerial behavior; it is important for a good manager to know how as well as to know that.

The Ethical Nature of Holistic Managing

This enlarged perspective of managing explicitly calls attention to a form of knowing that is alien to traditional analysis and that promotes a wider vision of managing and its associated concepts. According to the traditional analytic perspective, however, what is added here merely amounts to vague appeals to managerial style. However, the bifocal perspective of this chapter is unfairly criticized by glib references to style and personality. These concepts are more important than that and are significant for understanding the genuinely ethical nature of good management. Thus, the following section continues to explore what is meant by knowing how to manage, focusing on the ethics of managing and showing how management ethics is better understood as *management aesthetics*.

Traditionally, ethical knowledge was assumed to be analytic. This emphasis is accounted for in many ways, but perhaps the major reason was the dominating success of the natural sciences. Historically, this view of ethical knowledge was challenged by existential writers, like Kierkegaard, Nietzsche, and Sartre, who better appreciated the immediately subjective, holistic, and personal aspects of human awareness. But despite the positions of existential philosophers and the distinctions proposed in this chapter, ethical theory in general and business ethics in particular have been dominated by the analytic perspective. The twentieth century's seduction by techniques has been pervasive, and the attention given to the relation between ethical theory and business practice has been overwhelmingly analytic and procedure oriented.[10]

Recently, however, Charles Hartshorne has argued that the concept of ethics needs expansion. He asserts the importance of aesthetic categories for understanding ethics:

> . . . ethics must lean upon aesthetics. For the only good
> that is intrinsically good, good in itself, is good experi-

ence, and the criteria for this are aesthetic. Harmony and intensity come close to summing it up. . . . Intensity and beauty of experience, arising not only from visual or auditory stimuli, as a painting or music, but in experience of whatever sort, are what give life its value. *To be ethical is to seek aesthetic optimization of experience for · the community* [italics in the original].[11]

Alfred North Whitehead echoes this assertion when he writes, "Morality is always the aim at that union of harmony, intensity, and vividness which involves the perfection of importance for that occasion."[12] According to Hartshorne and Whitehead, then, ethics is fundamentally aesthetic, and the categories of right and wrong ultimately reduce to the beautiful and the ugly.

Many subtle human skills are genuinely ethical in the larger synthetic sense. Failure to perform yields bad results that otherwise could have been avoided by a manager with the holistic skills emphasized here. Whitehead once wrote: "Where attainable knowledge could have changed the issue, ignorance has the guilt of vice."[13] Here he is referring basically to forms of knowledge that illustrate the category of knowing that. However, his statement is easily generalized to include knowledge as knowing how. That is, "Where a ready smile," "Where firmness," "Where a bit of humor" could have changed the issue, *inability* has the guilt of vice. An unending list of human synthetic abilities seems relevant for promoting value and satisfaction among human beings. The sphere of ethical prescription is coterminous with the possibility of persons to produce beauty, to enhance lives, and to avoid ugliness. This may be especially true in management, where authority and power to promote such values are entrusted.

The analytic tradition of regarding ethics as primarily a matter of verbal justification rather than personal execution tends to hide important ethical and aesthetic issues behind words like *personality* and *style*. Consider the following vignette:

Your secretary, Joan Murphy, has worked faithfully for many years, and your friendship with her is of far greater personal value than can be measured by her competence.

Her behavior is sometimes idiosyncratic, and some think it odd, but you find it appealing. You would avoid hurting her feelings, if possible. It is now Monday morning, and Joan arrives at work wearing a hideous hat (in your opinion) and with pride in her eyes says, "Hi! How do you like my new hat?" What do you say?

From a traditional point of view, you are on the horns of a dilemma. It seems that you cannot avoid violating one of the ethical principles:

1.   Always tell the truth. (A formalistic requirement)
2.   You don't want to offend your friend. (A utilitarian concern)

Typical attempts to solve this problem are a little evasive:

"It's interesting."
"If you like it, I like it."
"It fits you, Joan."
"I wouldn't leave home without one."

However, when the people who first gave the preceding responses are then asked to reconsider from a very personal point of view, without trying to analyze the situation, their answers are different:

"It's lovely, Joan."
"You look terrific."

These people also sometimes reply that because of their interest in their secretary, they might also look for a more appropriate opportunity during the day to make more constructive comments, but only if it really mattered and only if the situation was right.

Now, what makes the difference in the two sets of responses? Are people generally either dishonest and evasive, on the one hand, or offensive, on the other?

When traditional analytic or linguistic categories dominate, when one is worried about consistency rather than constancy, when *speaking* the truth distracts attention from *being* true, the holistic or aesthetic nature of experience is reduced to a set of discrete components, sometimes creating difficult dilemmas, which on the holistic level are not problematic at all. And such synthetic episodes are experienced frequently by the typical administrator. They include such abilities as:

1. The ability to discharge an employee without promoting bitterness and contention
2. Selecting a team of compatible workers
3. Making exceptions to rules without abusing the rules
4. Instilling pride in subordinates' performance

Such skills involve style and can be attributed to personality, but it is not *merely* style and personality; these matters are *significant* and point to the relevance of aesthetic categories for understanding managerial behavior.

Thus, management ethics takes a broader than traditional look that allows us to see the ethical dimensions of competence, preparation, flexibility, and style. There are no decision procedures for these tasks; there are few useful rules. Such abilities demonstrate knowing how, not necessarily knowing that.

Art and Management

Successful management, therefore, consists of two forms of knowing—knowing that and knowing how—although the latter has, for good reasons, been emphasized in this chapter. Each form of knowledge complements the other. Thus, ethics becomes a successful balancing of the two forms of knowing. What results when this balance is achieved is genuinely aesthetic. Just as artists describe themselves as balancing form and content, repetition and novelty, light and dark, structure and detail, and so on, managers too balance opposed "pulls" in striving for truly ethical managerial competence.

Indeed, several writers have tried to show that managing is

a simultaneous balancing of opposed interests. Pascale and Athos, for example, discuss several pairs of balanced factors in their chapter on "Zen and the Art of Management":

rational	spiritual
control	autonomy
efficiency	human relations
short-term planner	long-term planner
obsession with facts	flexibility
authority	support
seniority	performance
monitor personnel	trust personnel
standardization	diversity[14]

With a little imagination, one can perceive the overall unity of the components of each group as illustrating elemental and contextual thinking, respectively. Thus, for Pascale and Athos, the art of managing is illustrated by successful managers around the world and consists of two types of knowing, as described here. This balancing is genuinely artistic. They add:

Observing a Matsushita controller deal with certain delicate situations provides an opportunity to study an art form. Carefully choosing his words, constructing a well-balanced tension between the general and the specific, the opaque and the clear, he picks his way across difficult terrain. Whether dealing with division managers before the planning group or with superintendents on the shop floor, he is always balancing.[15]

Similarly, in his book *The Gamesman*, Michael Maccoby describes the typical "gamesman" type of manager as being full of "seeming paradoxes":

He is idealistic, yet shrewd and pragmatic; cooperative, yet highly competitive; enthusiastic, yet detached; earnest, yet evasive; graceful, yet restless; energetic, yet itchy. Serious on the one hand, he is also boyish and playful with a twinkle in his eye.[16]

In *In Search of Excellence*, Peters and Waterman speak of *simultaneous loose–tight properties*, which they identify as a prime virtue of excellent companies. Their list looks like this:

1. efficiency   effectiveness
2. execution   autonomy
3. short-term   long-term
4. smart   dumb[17]

According to Peters and Waterman, the managing of paradox, as expressed in the list of loose–tight properties, is correlated with successful management. In the view of this chapter, tight properties are articulable, discrete, and a form of knowing that, while loose properties, a form of knowing how, indicate the need for ineffable skills and holistic thought. And both properties are of balanced importance to the successful manager. As R.M. Hare states,

> To say that it is impossible to keep intuitive and critical thinking going in the same thought process is like saying that in a battle a commander cannot at the same time be thinking of the details of the tactics, the overall aim of victory, and the principles (economy of force, concentration of force, offensive action, etc.) which he has learnt when learning his trade. Good generals do it.[18]

The urge to speak of managing in terms of simultaneous loose–tight properties, paradoxes, and balancing is contrasted with the traditional overemphasis on the tight, the rational and linguistic, the sequential, and it implies a growing awareness of the proper role of synthetic thinking, which can perhaps be described as more artistic. Being overly analytic, procedural, and bureaucratic in business relationships is similar to being the fake artist who "paints by the numbers": The holistic thought processes are absent, and what is produced satisfies the rules but is awkward and stiff. By analogy with music, the analytic reduction in managerial ethics is like the popular television game show "Name That Tune." A melody is extracted from a rich context of harmony and chord-progressions, and contestants are invited to guess the name of the tune from a short series of notes from the melody line. And if the contestants are often wrong in their guesses, by analogy the analytic reduction of ethics might make an interesting game, but it is bad ethics and bad management.

Implications for Ethical Theory

Good managing, therefore, is significantly aesthetic, and this accounts for the appeal of artistic categories in descriptions of management in current literature. It is a balancing of knowing how and knowing that. But good managing is also ethical managing—a balancing of utilitarian and formalistic orientations, as we have seen in earlier chapters. So, if we use these two dichotomous relations to produce a matrix, we should be able to focus in a little more graphically on good management practice.

Examining the matrix illustrated by the accompanying figure, the traditional expositions of utilitarian and formalistic ethical theory can be easily placed in quadrants 1 and 2, respectively. For decades, the explication of both theories has emphasized knowing that. Formalism has produced a view of ethics that sometimes appears dogmatic or legalistic, and utilitarianism likewise has placed excessive trust in a method of analysis. Both views, seen from the perspective of knowing that, have been characterized as unimaginative, sterile, cool,

	Utilitarianism	*Formalism*
Knowing that	1. policy analysis, technical comparison	2. legalistic, law-abiding
Knowing how	4. compassion, good will, general empathy	3. comfortably principled, reliable, consistent

Aesthetic Balancing in Ethics

minimal, tight, or just *empty* of the kinds of richness provided by experience that accompanies knowing how.

By contrast, the category of knowing that provides capacities for discrimination and insight, without which the category of knowing how becomes *blind*. In that case, utilitarianism is simply indiscriminate and individual acts of compassion without connectedness, and formalism is blind obedience or unquestioning cooperation, faithfulness, and obligation. Obviously, both compassion and obedience are important virtues, but they are not wholly virtuous without the direction and order supplied by careful analysis of the appropriate type. From the managerial point of view, we might say that quadrant 3 represents loyalty or cooperation without control or accounting and quadrant 4 represents enthusiasm, compassion, and willingness without plan or purpose. Both quadrants 3 and 4 are difficult to characterize because they represent inherently nonverbal forms of knowing to begin with.

But even more difficult to characterize are the midpoints in the matrix. Our language provides few words for these positions. We can use analogies, such as those mentioned in the following paragraph, to approximate and to allude to what is represented by a balanced approach in utilitarian and formalistic ethics.

Thus, at the balance of knowing that and knowing how, formalistic ethics looks at principles not as externally imposed requirements, but as admonishments that trigger greater attention to and proficiency in relating oneself appropriately to others, to the corporation, and to society. Our formal efforts to understand, to categorize, to systematize, and to order and arrange can be seen more as the reflective urgings, for example, of a voice teacher to a student — verbal instructions that are employed to trigger enhanced synthetic abilities, whether to vocalize a difficult vowel or to handle a complex situation with confidence and grace. Improved formal performance in managerial ethics is similar: It is a mature, critical trust in the value of norms and rules to secure cooperation, to promote self-discipline, and to broaden ethical awareness. This form of responsiveness to duty and to formal requirements is not a dull conforming that robs one of autonomy; on the contrary, it promotes sensitivity to human relationships and involves a

171

wide range of managerial skills. Hodgkinson's administrative principles or *propositions* explicitly illustrate this function of principles to "excite resonances" and "to act as a counterirritant against the compulsion towards behaviorism, denotation, and operational definition."[19]

Similarly, balancing the two forms of knowing for utilitarian concerns produces a mature, informed beneficence. Neither blind nor empty, the balanced utilitarian allows analysis to inform compassion and personal abilities to give substance and freshness to analytic rigor. Looked at in this way, the utilitarian decision procedure looks a little less like an algorithm and a little more like a graphic schema or checklist for maintaining and expanding the scope of one's awareness regarding the set of involved or interested persons and their wants and needs. It promotes an unflagging attention to diverse and competing goods and avoids premature closure and seduction of hasty conclusions.

Finally, the distinction between knowing that and knowing how reminds the administrator that there exist complementary forms of acquiring managerial knowledge. This is characteristic of the ethical perspective, as well as of a variety of other managerial concerns. And even though managers might hope to make their activities univocal and tightly rational, this wish may largely go unfulfilled. As Barrett says, "Policy-makers may only pretend to be technicians."[20]

Summary of Key Concepts

1. There are not one but two forms of knowing—knowing how to do something and knowing that something is so. The chief difference is verbal: Most things that we merely know how to do we cannot adequately describe.

2. Ethics, properly understood, draws on both forms of knowledge. In contrast to the rest of this book, this chapter examines the knowing how side of ethical behavior and its connection to knowing that.

3. On the holistic level, personal traits such as personality and style become critical for ethical behavior.

4. Competent managing is artistic because it balances the influence of knowing how and knowing that in decision-making processes. Thus, managing is part intuition and part deliberation.

5. Seeing from the perspective of knowing how, ethical theory (both utilitarianism and formalism) is empty; seeing from the perspective of knowing that, even the most inspired intuitive behavior is blind. The function of ethical theory for artful managing, therefore, is to supply at least some kind of insight into and rationale for acts that, at least in some measure, transcend such insights.

Questions and Exercises

1. Art is a highly creative activity. How is ethical managing also creative?

2. Art in the twentieth century has generally been described as an unrestrained experimentation with materials and media. Has management experienced a similar explosive experimentation?

3. Review the Pascale and Athos example in Chapter Two. What aesthetic elements might be important in resolving such a confrontation?

4. Robert Pirsig a few years ago wrote a best-selling novel called *Zen and the Art of Motorcycle Maintenance*. It is an investigation into the nature of quality. Inside the front cover, Pirsig wrote: "The real cycle you're working on is a cycle called 'yourself.' The study of the art of motorcycle maintenance is really a miniature study of the art of rationality itself. Working on a motorcycle, working well, caring, is to become part of a process, to achieve an inner peace of mind. The motorcycle is primarily a mental phenomenon." Substitute *administration* for *the motorcycle* in this quotation, and evaluate the new statement for its relevance to this chapter.

5. In an article titled "The Technology of Foolishness" (in *Ambiguity and Choice in Organizations* by James March and Johan Olsen, printed in Bergen by Universitetsforlaget, 1976, pp. 69–81), March makes the following observations:

   Consider, for example, the difficulty of sustaining playfulness as a style within contemporary American society. Individuals who are good at consistent rationality are rewarded early and heavily. We define it as intelligence, and the educational rewards of society are associated strongly with it. Social norms press in the same direction, particularly for men. Many of the demands of modern organizational life reinforce the same abilities and style preferences.

The result is that many of the most influential, best educated, and best placed citizens have experienced a powerful overlearning with respect to rationality. . . .

Which form of knowing does March refer to when he speaks of *rationality*? What form of knowing is implied in his reference to *playfulness*? Is he correct in asserting that we have "overlearned" one form of knowing at the expense of the other?

C H A P T E R

9

Football, Sharks, and Warfare — The Challenge to Ethical Theory

We began this book by making a distinction between matters of the heart and matters of the head. We return to that distinction in this chapter.

What we promised in Chapter Two was an examination of business ethics as a matter of the mind. Ethics as a matter of the heart is more appropriately the concern of the clergy or of a parent; it is less connected to academic expertise. So, as promised, this book has focused on *thinking* about ethics and what that means for business administrators, whose role is as much to justify their decisions as to make them.

Consequently, the reader has by now sensed that this book is a little more detached, a little more academic and less "earthy," perhaps, than may have been expected. One might have hoped to find exposés, inspiring exhortations, uplifting insights, condemnations, or lists of practical suggestions for changes in behavior. Instead, what has been provided is a collection of exploratory ideas for improving deliberation in complex ethical issues. Indeed, this book is about matters of the head rather than the heart.

But just because this Janus-headed model of ethical theory can be described as "administrative" or "academic," don't confuse that with "irrelevant." Ethical administration is deliberate, complex, rational, thoughtful, and objective; it is also much more. And although I can provide little evidence for it other than personal testimony, I believe that the forms of thinking discussed in this book complement and sustain all the proper heartfelt responses that are consistent with human administrative maturity.

Although the connection of the claims of this book with matters of the heart is the subject of yet another book, there is some evidence for the strength of that connection in a contrast with a familiar but ethically inferior competing perspective regarding business behavior. As far as I can tell, this view has not been named or systematically investigated, although it is pervasive in popular business "how to" manuals. It stands as the chief adversary of the view propounded in this book, and despite its popularity, it can be demonstrated, I think, to be ethically repulsive. By contrast with the Janus-headed analogy, we will call it the *game analogy*.

The purpose of this chapter is to develop and examine the game analogy, provide illustrations of its impact on business behavior, demonstrate its ethical inconsistency, and connect it to a supporting ideology. In the process, we shall see how the game analogy sustains a particular set of human dispositions, wants, and motives. And we shall show how these motives contrast sharply with those dispositions, or matters of the heart, that are characteristic of the ethical theoretic orientation proposed in this book.

The Game Analogy of Business Behavior

In 1968 Albert Carr wrote an article that has often been reprinted and included in collections of business ethics essays. Its primary purpose seemed to be to defend "business bluffing." The article began by quoting a statement made by Henry Taylor, an English statesman, who said, "Falsehood ceases to be falsehood when it is understood on all sides that the truth is not expected to be spoken."[1] In short, the activities of business are regulated not by any objective or externally imposed set of standards but by whatever rules the participants agree to accept. Therefore, lying becomes bluffing so long as everyone playing the game of business understands at the outset that such behavior is allowed and even expected. Carr, therefore, tried to argue for the acceptability of regarding business activity as a set of economic behaviors that was self-defining, self-regulating, and independent of norms and standards that might be in force for other social activities external to the business game.

Indeed, Carr's primary analogy for business behavior was poker. Poker is a narrow form of economic behavior with its own rules, and different rules may be adopted by the players from game to game. Throughout, bluffing is not only allowed but is an essential skill and is greatly respected. Those who win at poker, those who play the best, are most commonly those who bluff the best. Telling the truth is at best irrelevant. Carr says, for example, "Whatever the form of the bluff, it is an integral part of the game, and the executive who does not master its techniques is not likely to accumulate much money or power."[2]

This game analogy for business activity is appealing in that it can be further developed. It is a stronger analogy than Carr wrote about, and it serves well as a descriptive account of much business behavior. Frank Knight, for example, pointed out three important features common to business and games: skill, effort, and luck. He argued that luck was perhaps the most significant of the three.[3]

Other features of the model are easily added. For example, in many games or sports, violation of the rules is acceptable unless one is caught. In basketball, for instance, good coaches "work" the referees, and players bluff or fake defenders and seek to gain the favor of the referees while at the same time disguising fouls or other violations of the rules from them. Therefore, there are two sets of game rules: one set that defines the parameters of the game and a somewhat different set that describes the attitudes and expectations of the players.

The existence of the second set of informal rules is a consequence of the attempt by players to seize advantage where they can. If a game rule is clear but difficult to enforce, players will commonly exploit the limitations of the referees, creating a differential between the referees' expectations and those of the players. If the game rule is too difficult to monitor or enforce, players will certainly exploit the weakness, resulting in game behavior that may not be preferred by the players, the officials, or anyone else. Basketball, for example, is supposed to be a noncontact sport. But if the officiating is weak or passive, behavior can degenerate to a form of play that everyone accepts but no one necessarily enjoys.

The analogy, of course, is seen in business behavior. "Officiating," or regulation, is weakest on the international level. Here various forms of ethically marginal behavior occur, including the dumping in a foreign country of products that were banned at home, the sale of military arms, bribery, and exploitation of cheap labor. In all such cases, the most common excuse is "Everybody else does it; why can't I?" or "If we don't, somebody else will." Such excuses reflect the existence of a game-like set of expectations among the various "players" that may differ considerably from norms and expectations of social contact outside the game of international business.

So, the game analogy of business behavior seems to be an adequate heuristic device. Obviously, it has not been fully developed here, but some of the points of analogy would include these:

1. The existence of a set of rules independent of other forms of social behavior

2. The existence of expectations for behavior among the players that differ from the formal set of rules governing play

3. The need to satisfy the referees, as opposed to satisfying the rules of the game

4. The existence of some forms of behavior that are the product of intense competition combined with weakness of regulation

It would be worthwhile to develop further the analogy between games and business activity. For one thing, it would include examining a variety of games to see which ones approach and which differ from business behavior. "Monopoly," for example, which is explicitly designed to mimic the business world, may in fact be a poor reflection, while football may provide the closest analogy of all.

In his recent book *Moral Mazes*, Robert Jackall argues that "of all major sports, football resonates most deeply with managers' preferred image of what they do."[4] He adds that the jargon of football has found its way into managerial usage, and he provides a list of such phrases together with their metaphorical meaning for business managers:

Players	Anyone who has a stake in and is therefore involved in a decision
Carrying the ball	Responsible for an assignment
Taking the ball and running with it	Showing initiative and drive
Fumbling the ball	Messing up an assignment
Passing the ball	Getting rid of a responsibility
Punt	Employ a defensive strategy while waiting for things to sort out
Sidelined	Getting taken out of the game; benched
Run the clock down	Wear out an opponent by stalling
Huddle	A quick meeting
Reverse or reversing fields	Changing one's story or public rationale for an action; changing strategies
Going over the top	Achieving one's commitments
Running interference or blocking	A patron using personal influence to knock down opposition to a client's ideas or plans
Broken field run	A virtuoso individual performance
Getting blindsided	Being unexpectedly undercut by another in public
Quarterback	The boss

Jackall also lists five rules for "team play." They are:

1. One must appear to be interchangeable with other managers near one's level. (Idiosyncratic managers are too unpredictable.)

2. One must be willing to put in long hours at the office.

3. One must be seen as an effective group member, performing one's assigned tasks without appearing to be a prima donna.

4. One must align oneself with the dominant ideology of the moment.

5. One must display a happy, upbeat, can-do approach to one's work and to the organization.[5]

So, the game of business is played on a scale as large as international business and as small as office politics. The common feature is that business activity (large or small) is regarded as a competitive, self-contained game with its own rules and without significant implications beyond the success or failure of the players. It is assumed that those who play agree to play "by the rules." And those rules may reflect behaviors that are not normally accepted in the wider social context. For example, in football, players tackle, block, and in general engage in behavior similar to, but just short of, open fighting; it is allowed for purposes of the game.

Likewise, the application of the game analogy in business apparently allows behaviors that may not be acceptable in a wider social context. If the game analogy of business activity were merely a descriptive device that enabled us to perceive and understand the range of business behaviors more fully, we might not feel quite so bothered by it. But it is used for more than that. It serves also as a prescriptive tool: "If you want to play the game, you'll play our way," and so on. So the game analogy challenges the authority of the Janus-headed view of ethical theory by warranting almost any kind of behavior, so long as it conforms to the rules of the game and all players are aware of the rules, whether those rules and behaviors conform to the canons of ethical theory or not.

A fuller, more systematic development of the game analogy of business behavior would be very useful. In lieu of a richer analytic treatment, however, it might be more interesting to provide several concrete illustrations of just what the game analogy allows in the way of business behavior.

Examples of Game Behaviors in Business

Robert Jackall concludes his recent sociological monograph on business managerial behaviors with the following insight:

> The ethos that they [those who succeed] fashion turns principles into guidelines, ethics into etiquette, values into tastes, personal responsibility into an adroitness at public relations, and notions of truth into credibility. Corporate managers who become inbued with this ethos pragmatically take their world as they find it and try to make that world work according to its own institutional logic. They pursue their own careers and good fortunes as best they can within the rules of their world. As it happens, given their pivotal institutional role in our epoch, they help create and re-create, as one unintended consequence of their personal striving, a society where morality becomes indistinguishable from the quest for one's own survival and advantage.[6]

Jackall's argument is, in part, that much or most behavior in the business world follows the game model, with its own internal logic or rules of the game. As a consequence, norms and strategies for success differ not only from prescriptions in the previous century but also from the normal set of expectations that currently comprise other institutional logics, such as those of the family, school, neighborhood, religion, and so on. A review of some of these norms and recommendations might help more than a systematic analysis to clarify the applied nature of the game model of business.

Short-Term Decision Making

Because promotions, reorganizations, and changes of assignment occur with great frequency in business, managers' thinking is necessarily short-term. The next promotion will come from making one's boss look good and therefore increasing his or her chances of promotion; and one looks good in the short run or even in the present. Therefore, most decisions are made to make one's boss look good, and you hope for the sake of those you supervise that they, in turn, are performing so as to make you look good as well.

One way of describing successful managers is to say they outrun their mistakes. They move fast enough from job to job so that their mistakes never catch up with them. But mistakes are being made. Therefore, one's greatest fear is that one will be in the wrong place at the wrong time and inherit the consequences of a predecessor's mistakes.

Recent victories and successes are the stuff of promotions. By the same token, one recent mistake can overshadow a history of consistent performance. Therefore, managerial decision-making behavior is conservative and participatory: It is conservative because you don't want to make any decision unless it is unavoidable, and it is participatory because the more people involved in a decision the easier it is to absolve oneself of responsibility if something goes wrong and to cast the blame elsewhere.

A typical illustration of how short-term decision making affects an organization is found in a practice commonly referred to as *milking* or *starving* a plant. It consists of maximizing one's return on assets (ROA) for the quarter or the fiscal year. The most common way of milking a plant is to defer capital investments as long as possible while maintaining sales. Consequently, as one's assets are reduced, the ROA figures look better and better. Of course, over the long term, this strategy is often disastrous; but because of managerial mobility, one is seldom concerned about the long term. Someone else will inherit those problems. It would be stupid game strategy to try to do things now that will make the team look good when you are gone. At that time, you might even be on a competing team! One manager says:

> We're judged on the short-term because everybody changes their jobs so frequently. As long as we have a system where I'm told that I am not going to be in a job for the long term, you're going to have this pressure. And you're not tracked from one job to the next, so you can milk your present situation and never have it pinned on you in the future. . . . Essentially, when I think of milking a business, I think of shutting off any

capital expenditure and anything that is an expense. And you know what happens when you do that? The guy who comes into that mess is the one who gets blamed, not the guy who milked it.[7]

So, one important feature of business activity perceived as a game is short-term decision making, which is largely a consequence of managerial mobility and loyalty to one's boss. If the end of the game is personal success, and if that in turn is defined by frequent promotions, evaluation according to some other long-term or objective standards serves little purpose.

Expediency

If managing is to be regarded as a game with purposes and goals independent of the rest of living, then anything that serves those ends or purposes becomes the expedient thing to do. Consequently, almost anything can come to be regarded as instrumental in the game, including things that might otherwise be seen as intrinsically good or bad.

In the first case, friendships are certainly cultivated in the business world, but such friendships tend to be described in terms of loyalty, team membership, and allegiance. They cease to be good in themselves and instead are regarded as good for business game strategy. As one manager reported:

> Our motives are purely selfish. We're not concerned about old Joe failing, but we're worried about how his failure will reflect on us. When you pick somebody, say, you invest part of yourself in him. So his failure and what it means to his kids and so on mean nothing. . . . [8]

So, although a friendship in other circumstances might be thought of as intrinsically satisfying, in the business world friendships can be distorted to serve other purposes.

Another recently published "how to" manual in business describes some tactics that are tailor-made for use against peers when you decide that they are in your way. Called *political euthanasia*, these are suggested actions for bringing about a hasty exit: creating obstacles, the veiled cut, the setup, rais-

ing ambiguity, emotional blackmail, repetition, change, carp-
ing, and "terror and the veiled cut."[9] One suggestion, for
example, is to "feed someone the wrong information ... [so
that] he/she subsequently blunders into a fight with the
work processing supervisor or the manager of information
systems."[10]

The same author reminds us:

> Genuine friendships in the office are unlikely, and even
> hazardous to your career. This doesn't mean you should
> be misanthropic, just be watchful. Everyone's primary
> duty is to stay on the payroll. . . . Friendship is fleeting.
> Each worker's first responsibility is to defend his job
> and enlarge it. . . . There is no such thing as "fair" in
> business. Any tactic you can get away with that is legal
> and reasonably ethical is all right and may even be
> grudgingly admired by those who aren't as successful.[11]

Lying and Deception

Furthermore, a wide variety of questionable behavior can be
regarded as acceptable under the rules of the game. For
instance, lying and deception ordinarily are regarded as improper behavior but are even recommended in some business
circles. A recent best-selling business success book urges the
following:

> Let's say you're entertaining customers in a town
> where you don't belong to a club. How do you give
> yourself the patina of respectability a club imparts and
> create that cozy, clublike atmosphere in a place where
> nobody knows you?
> Easy.
> The best way, of course, is to get someone you know
> in town to let you use their club and sign a tab in the
> member's name. That's a whale of an imposition, but if
> you have a friend willing to let you do it, do it.[12]

The same author urges various forms of deception, especially
when negotiating a deal. For instance, he recites an "ancient

scam" in the car business known as "Calling Mr. Otis." He describes it this way:

> The sales person writes up the deal. He has the pros-
> pect initial it. Then he asks the prospect casually what
> the other dealers offered him. At this point, the pros-
> pect, flushed with victory, tosses away the most valuable
> asset he has in the negotiation: information — to wit, the
> other dealers' prices.
> "Just one last step," says the salesperson. "The sales
> manager has to okay the deal. I'll call him right now.
> . . . The sales manager [Mr. Otis] shows up. He pulls
> the salesman out of the room to let the prospect stew
> for a while, the salesman comes back, says Otis won't go
> for the deal, and then proceeds to retrade it up to
> exactly the same level the other dealers had offered the
> prospect.[13]

Of course, there is no Mr. Otis. That is just the signal for cooperation in deceiving the unsuspecting customer. But the deception is described as a recommended strategy by the author, who claims to offer insights into the real world of business.

Thus, lying and deception cease to exist as antisocial be-haviors and, instead, come to be regarded as allowed or even expected behavior under the rules. As one manager put it, "We lie all the time, but if everyone knows that we're lying, is a lie really a lie?"[14]

We could dwell at length on typical behaviors that illustrate the kinds of things that are often allowed in business under the rules of the game, but perhaps the foregoing is enough to indicate their general flavor and variety. Any doubts concern-ing this characterization of business as a game, or that a report like Jackall's is too cynical, are dispelled by finding the same behaviors recommended in popular business "how to" manuals by those who claim to have special insight into the business world or to have experienced business success. The game anal-ogy of business behavior is pervasive, even if it conflicts with alternative views of business behavior, including the Janus-headed analogy.

The Game Analogy of Business and Ethical Theory

Throughout this book, we have tended to examine the implication of ethical theory for the larger standard business-society issues. In general, our treatment of business ethics has been oriented to policy, as opposed to individual and organizational behavior issues.

But ethical theory is relevant for all levels of ethical analysis—abstract or concrete, macro or micro, organizational or individual. This includes the kinds of behavior previously explored. Contrary to what is claimed by the game model of business behavior, we will show how business cannot regard itself as a gamelike exception to the usual standards of behavior and how the forms of behavior reviewed earlier are not protected from ethical criticism on the grounds that they are part of a game.

Ethical Formalism and the Game of Business

The primary defense of business behavior as game behavior calls upon the independence of game rules from normal rules or behavior. Poker, boxing, ice hockey, and betting at the race track are all examples of games or sports that institutionalize forms of behavior otherwise thought unacceptable in the normal social context: lying, battery, fighting, and gambling. Other sports, such as football, wrestling, and karate, legitimize behaviors that might be questioned under other circumstances.

If business activity is sufficiently similar to game behavior, then formalism will by its own requirements approve such business activities. Universalizability requires that like actions be treated alike ethically; and if business behavior indeed *is* gamelike, then ethical theory can no more criticize standard business behaviors than it can criticize the rules of sports or games. Everything depends on the strength of the analogy.

The formalistic attack on the game analogy of business behavior can proceed in two ways: First, it can show the analogy between business behaviors and games to be faulty. Second, it can provide an alternative, stronger analogy to take the place of the game model. Both strategies will now be pursued.

Weakness of the Game Analogy One way in which business activity is unlike games relates to the seriousness of the consequences for success or failure. In most games, success or failure is as independent of the rest of living as are the rules of the games themselves. Failure at a game does not usually threaten one's well-being or ability to supply basic needs. Failure at business, on the other hand, can be serious, resulting in change of location or even bankruptcy, and stress or trauma to one's life in a variety of ways.

Business also differs from the typical game in terms of one's freedom to play or not to play. Although it is reasonable to suppose that the rules of the game, or corporate culture, vary from firm to firm, requiring a person to move from job to job in search of an acceptable culture may not be so reasonable. If the forms of game behavior described previously are pervasive in a community or in an industry, the individual's choice to play may be a very narrow one.

In defense of the game analogy, it might be argued that people sense quite early in life the general features of the various economic games available to them, and they make early selections regarding the acceptability of the general field of work, making only much later the specific decisions regarding jobs and locations. Thus, they are self-determined and do make choices regarding which business games to play, although the choices are somewhat irreversible. However, such early choices are not always well informed. It is common among academicians, for example, to dislike teaching simply because, although they like their subject, they never experienced teaching until after making a deep commitment to pursue the Ph.D. Law students, sales personnel, and musicians sometimes have similar experiences, failing to anticipate the consequences of their choices. So, these reasonings suggest that finding oneself immersed in business behaviors not to one's liking may not be the result of informed choice. And cooperating in such forms of behavior is not so casual as a preference regarding the use of leisure time.

An Alternative Analogy Instead of thinking of business culture as a game, a closer analogy might be a teenager. Consider the following points of analogy between teenagers and businesses:

1. They are strong and vigorous.
2. They often test the rules with challenging behavior.
3. They are irresponsible.
4. They are experimental.
5. They are capable of getting into trouble and acquiring bad habits.
6. They may become adults.
7. They have acne (or other forms of blemishes).
8. They need to establish their own identities and achieve success.
9. They care about how they look.

The strength of this casual analogy leads us to suppose that business in America is not quite mature, provokes paternalistic regulation, and rebels against external control. This is a useful analogy, but it is more fun than serious.

At the turn of the century, a more serious analogy was proposed by Herbert Spencer. The analogy was to evolutionary concepts, and it came to be known as *social Darwinism*. According to social Darwinism, business activity is no game. It is a struggle of the fittest to survive in a hostile environment. Spencer proposed simply that businesses "fight it out" without government interference. Government was regarded as an intrusion into natural processes that, if left alone over the long run, would produce more vigorous social institutions than could be promoted by any other form of nurturing or intervention.[15] Applying the same principles that Charles Darwin saw in biological life, this view of social and economic interaction became quite popular.

If social Darwinism is a reasonable analogy for describing business behavior, the idea that business is a game is seen in a clearer light: The game analogy becomes a euphemism for business behavior that, from a moral perspective, is just normal animal behavior; that is, it is amoral. The problem, of course, with the analogy to social Darwinism is that human beings are not merely animals; we are also moral beings. And if our interactions seem well described by social Darwinian concepts, we can only conclude that we are acting like animals when we should be acting, instead, like human beings. Therefore, the game analogy is not only a poor analogy for business behavior, it casts a veneer of approval on activities that may be far less than what they could be or should be.

So, from the perspective of ethical formalism, the game analogy of business activity seems suspect as a justification for much of the activity that various authors have pointed out or even recommended. Since the primary rule of the game is to seize the advantage, to get ahead, an ethical perspective such as formalism, which emphasizes universalizable acts, will hardly approve the game, especially if getting ahead happens at the expense of others.

Traditionally, the game is thought to be justifiable on utilitarian grounds: Many human actions and institutions are universalizable, but not all. Human beings have differences, too, and those differences are important as cooperative contributions to an improved world. Perhaps the seizing of advantage can be attached to forms of competition that result in overall growth, production, and the general welfare.

Utilitarianism and Business Competition

So, the traditional charter for general business activity appeals to utilitarian grounds: The general welfare is served by sustained economic activity and the kind of growth and efficiency of production that are fostered by competitive enterprise. Adam Smith's appeal to the *invisible hand* of the free market is the charter metaphor for allowing business activity more or less complete freedom.

Of course, free enterprise is vulnerable to the criticism that the distribution of costs and benefits is unfair, but it is not our purpose here to pursue a general criticism of business activity — only a criticism of those business activities participating in the syndrome of behaviors outlined earlier in this chapter, such as conspiracies, decision avoidance, scapegoating, milking, and so on.

To begin with, it seems reasonable enough to assume that not all kinds of business activity can be justified by an appeal to economic or utilitarian ends. It is difficult to argue, for example, that cigarette production and sales serve utilitarian ends. An even clearer but related example might be the sale of controlled substances. In the latter case, we have decided that the product causes far more harm than the good that might accrue to an economy through the revenue created from sales. Healthy, diverse economies generally find ways to take up the slack when some industry falters. (For this reason, I have never been too interested in the "loss of jobs" argument often used by those who want to defend continued production or sale of useless or harmful products, such as cigarettes or marijuana.)

But the most focused question is: "Does the short-term competitive syndrome of behaviors outlined earlier serve any utilitarian purposes that could not be better served by some alternative arrangement?" Another way of putting this is to ask: "Does business life have to be mean and nasty?" The answer to this question is probably empirical rather than conceptual. If optimal production in terms of both quantity and quality can be secured only through the form of business activity described earlier as the game model, then there exists a trade-off between the process and the product of business activity. And we will have to decide which is more important.

But there is reason to believe that optimal production does not require a game analogy environment. Some games involving teams, in fact, secure individual and team success through cooperation instead of internal competition. Baseball players, for example, are not known for withholding their advice from younger up-and-coming players; on the contrary, they act as mentors, even when the younger players threaten to take their jobs away. Cooperation, sharing, mentoring, and teaching in such cases are part of what is meant by *professional*; less team-oriented behavior is described as *bush league*. Furthermore, organizational processes in other countries do not necessarily share the game analogy features of the United States. Employment for a business manager in Japan, for example, is more secure than in the United States. Pascale and Athos describe it in terms of *coordinated interdependence*.[16]

My personal impression of the game analogy behavior described earlier is that it is extraordinarily selfish. "Looking out for number one" can be found in any institutionalized setting—the university, the home, the neighborhood, church, and so on. That it may be more common in business cannot be excused by standard appeals to private vices that yield public virtues. Selfishness violates utilitarian principles; in fact, it is probably the most common reason for failing to meet utilitarian requirements. It secures one person's benefit at the expense of others. And institutionalized selfishness may sacrifice a great deal for the bottom line. Criteria for business success that are so narrow as to ignore all factors other than personal promotability fail elementary utilitarian analysis.

More specifically, such behavior violates the prohibition on spatial proximity described in Chapter Five. Personal promotability is used as a dominant criterion when there are probably other criteria that, even if considered alone, would serve better: organizational success, hard work, productivity, team success, and so on. And the predominant focus on short-term rather than long-term success violates the prohibition on temporal proximity. In short, the here-and-now orientation in organizational behavior is clearly contrary to basic utilitarian principles. If anything is gained in the aggregate (Adam Smith's invisible hand argument), it is a sad commentary on human nature: That happiness and success should proceed magically from systematic individual selfish acts ignores standard religious wisdom and higher human virtues. "Survival of the fittest" may be a scientific way to account for unintentional physiological progress, but it is a useless metaphor for describing the intended progress of civilization. Jon Elster describes the necessity of cooperation this way: "In a population of peaceful organisms an aggressive mutant will get the upper hand, but its descendants may peck each other to death."[17]

Milking plants, deceiving clients, puffing one's own image, manipulating and using one's peers, covering up problems, and glorifying one's boss are all business behaviors that are recommended in "how to" manuals for business success on the grounds that that's the way the game is played. Indeed, recent sociological accounts of the moral context of managerial life in the business world bear out many of these claims: these manuals might as well be rule books for the game of business. And that's too bad, because it's difficult to see how such behavior, no matter how pervasive, can be justified on any ethical grounds.

What this analysis begins to point to, I think, is a general compatibility between ethical theory and some of the civilized virtues, such as honesty, cooperation, kindness, and friendship. Our general distaste for game analogy business behavior arises from more than an incompatibility with ethical theory; we *feel* the moral distance as well. So, we have come full circle from Chapter Two. We are now prepared to examine matters of the heart in business behavior, seeing, perhaps, that the heart and the mind may agree on their findings.

Summary of Key Concepts

1. The most commonly used metaphor for business activity is the game. The most common game used to describe business activity is football.

2. This game analogy is used to defend a variety of ethically questionable business behaviors on the grounds that it is all part of the game of business. Such behaviors include short-term decision making, mere expediency, and various forms of lying and deception.

3. The game analogy is unethical for both formalistic and utilitarian reasons. The formalist reminds us that business is more serious than a game; alternative analogies come closer. The utilitarian sees gamelike behavior as selfish and fails to see how aggregated selfish behaviors add up to anything but generalized selfishness.

Questions and Exercises

1. It is often thought that business is one thing and ethics is
    another, allowing success in winning at the business game
    to be unrestrained by ethics and restrained by the law only
    when caught. What comes first—being a person or being
    a business person?

2. What is the difference between bluffing and deception in
    a high-stakes game of poker, for example, and the bluff-
    ing and deception of a car salesperson?

3. Consider the following case: Suppose you were touring a
    small candy manufacturing plant that you owned, and
    from a distance you saw an employee insert an insect into
    one of the pieces of candy. Before you could bring the
    process to a halt, hundreds of pieces of candy had been
    made, and the one with the insect was somewhere in the
    batch but you did not know where.
    a. What would you do?
    b. What would you do if the object were a razor blade
        instead of an insect?
    c. What would you do if it were mixed in with 1,000
        pieces rather than 100?
    d. What would you do if no one but you saw or sus-
        pected the contamination of the candy?

4. Can friendships thrive in the context of a game only? If
    business is only a game, are friendships common relation-
    ships, or is one more likely to find something else—tem-
    porary allegiances, dependencies, and so on?

5. It is often difficult to shut down or restrain production of
    questionable products because jobs will be lost. Of course,
    it is important for people to have work, but does that
    mean just any kind of work? Is the kind of work a person
    does important? Should one be concerned about what
    kind of product a company produces in deciding whether
    to accept a job with that company?

Endnotes

Chapter Two

1. M. Novak, *The Spirit of Democratic Capitalism* (New York: Simon & Schuster, 1982).

2. William Barrett, *The Illusion of Technique* (Garden City, N.Y.: Anchor Press, Doubleday, 1979), p. 25.

3. Ludwig Wittgenstein, *Philosophical Investigations*, 3rd ed. (New York: Macmillan, 1958), p. 38.

4. Lawrence Kohlberg, "Stage and Sequence: The Cognitive-Developmental Approach to Socialization, in D. A. Goslin (ed.), *Handbook of Socialization: Theory and Research* (Chicago: Rand-McNally, 1969), pp. 347–480.

5. P. Grim, L. Kohlberg, and S. White, "Some Relationships Between Conscience and Attentional Processes," *Journal of Personality and Social Psychology*, V. 8 (1968), pp. 239–252.

6. S. McNamee, "Moral Behavior, Moral Development, and Motivation, *Journal of Moral Education*, V. 7 (1977), pp. 27–31.

7. D. Krebs and A. Rosenwald, "Moral Reasoning and Moral Behavior in Conventional Adults," *Merrill Palmer Quarterly*, V. 23 (1977), pp. 77–87.

8. L. Trevino, "Ethical Decision Making in Organizations: A Person–Situation Interactionist Model," *Academy of Management Review*, V. 11 (1986), pp. 601–617.

9. S. Milgram, "A Behavioral Study of Obedience," *Journal of Abnormal and Social Psychology*, V. 67 (1963), pp. 371–378.

10. J. Darley and C. Batson, "From Jerusalem to Jericho: A Study of Situational and Dispositional Variables in Helping Behavior," *Journal of Personality and Social Psychology*, V. 27 (1973), pp. 100–108.

11. C. Haney, C. Banks, and P. Zimbardo, "Interpersonal Dynamics in a Simulated Prison," *International Journal of Criminology and Penology*, V. 1 (1973), pp. 69–97.

12. A. MacIntyre, *After Virtue*, 2nd ed. (Notre Dame, Ind.: Notre Dame University Press, 1984), p. 165.

13. A. MacIntyre.

14. E. Pincoffs, *Quandaries and Virtues: Against Reductivism in Ethics* (Lawrence, Kan.: University of Kansas Press, 1986).

15. R. Pascale and A. Athos, *The Art of Japanese Management* (New York: Warner Books, 1981).

16. E. Pincoffs, p. 27.

17. R. Pascale and A. Athos, pp. 136–137.

18. A. N. Whitehead, *Modes of Thought* (New York: Free Press, 1938), p. 11.

Chapter Three

1. Aristotle, *The Ethics of Aristotle*, J. A. K. Thomson, trans. (London: Allen & Unwin, 1953).

2. J. Bentham, *An Introduction to the Principles of Morals and Legislation* (Oxford: Clarendon Press, 1897) (originally published in 1789).

3. A. MacIntyre, "Utilitarianism and Cost-Benefit Analysis: An Essay on the Relevance of Moral Philosophy to Bureaucratic Theory," in K. Sayer (ed.), *Values in the Electric Power Industry* (Notre Dame, Ind.: Notre Dame University Press, 1977), p. 224.

4. U. LeGuin, "The Ones Who Walk Away from Omelas," in M. Greenberg (ed.), *Fantasy Hall of Fame* (New York: Arbor House, 1983).

5. A. Kaplan, *The Conduct of Inquiry* (San Francisco: Chandler, 1964), p. 11.

6. I. Hoos, *Systems Analysis in Public Policy*, rev. ed. (Los Angeles: University of California Press, 1983), p. 248 (first edition published in 1972).

7. F. Copleston, *A History of Philosophy* (Garden City, N.Y.: Doubleday, 1964), V. 6, p. 209.

8. F. Copleston, p. 212.

9. I. Kant, *Critique of Practical Reason*, L. W. Beck, trans. (New York: Bobbs-Merrill, 1956), p. 30 (originally published in 1788).

10. For a philosophical presentation of these ideas, see John Rawls, "Two Concepts of Rules," *Philosophical Review*, V. 64 (1955), pp. 3–32.

Chapter Four

In an earlier form, this chapter was published as "A Janus-Headed Model of Ethical Theory: Looking Two Ways at Business/Society Issues," *The Academy of Management Review*, V. 10 (1985), pp. 568–576.

1. S. Bok, *Secrets: On the Ethics of Concealment and Revelation* (New York: Random House, 1983).

2. M. S. Baram, "Trade Secrets: What Price Loyalty?" *Harvard Business Review*, V. 46 (1968), pp. 66–74.

3. S. Bok, "Whistleblowing and Professional Responsibility," *New York University Education Quarterly*, V. 2 (1980), pp. 2–7.

4. See R. DeGeorge, "Can Corporations Have Moral Responsibility?" in T. L. Beauchamp and N. E. Bowie (eds.), *Ethical Theory and Business* (Englewood Cliffs, N.J.: Prentice-Hall, 1979); and A. F. Westin, "What Can and Should Be Done to Protect Whistleblowers in Industry?" in A. F. Westin (ed.), *Whistleblowing: Loyalty and Dissent in the Corporation* (New York: McGraw-Hill, 1981).

5. N. Bowie, "When in Rome, Should You Do as the Romans Do?" in T. Beauchamp and N. Bowie (eds.), *Ethical Theory and Business*, 2nd ed. (Englewood Cliffs, N.J.: Prentice-Hall, 1983), pp. 276–279.

6. R. T. DeGeorge, *Business Ethics*, 2nd ed. (New York: Macmillan, 1986, p. 63.

7. W. T. Blackstone, "Ethics and Ecology," in W. T. Blackstone (ed.), *Philosophy and the Environmental Crisis* (Athens: University of Georgia Press, 1974), pp. 16–42; J. Feinberg, "The Rights of Animals and Unborn Generations," in W. T. Blackstone (ed.), *Philosophy and the Environmental Crisis*; and C. Stone, *Where the Law Ends* (New York: Harper & Row, 1975).

8. W. T. Blackstone, p. 19.

9. G. A. Sojka, "Where Biology Could Take Us," *Business Horizons*, V. 24 (1981), pp. 60–69.

10. C. Mills, "Not with a Bang: The Moral Perplexities of Nuclear Deterrence," *Report from the Center for Philosophy and Public Policy*, V. 3 (1983), pp. 1–5.

11. See R. T. DeGeorge, 1986, pp. 82–100; K. Goodpaster and J. Matthews, "Can a Corporation Have a Conscience?" *Harvard Business Review*, V. 60 (1982), pp. 132–141; and J. Ladd, "Morality and the Ideal of Rationality in Formal Organizations," *Monist*, V. 54 (1970), pp. 488–516.

12. G. Bateson, *Mind and Nature: A Necessary Unity* (New York: E. P. Dutton, 1979), p. 222.

13. A. MacIntyre, "Utilitarianism and Cost-Benefit Analysis: An Essay on the Relevance of Moral Philosophy to Bureaucratic Theory," in K. Sayer (ed.), *Values in the Electric Power Industry* (Notre Dame, Ind.: Notre Dame University Press, 1977), pp. 217–237.

14. See K. Marx, "The Ideology of Capitalism," in T. B. Bottomore (ed.), *Karl Marx: Selected Writings in Sociology and Social Psychology* (New York: McGraw-Hill, 1964) (originally published in 1845); L. Tribe, "Technology Assessment and the Fourth Discontinuity: The Limits of Instrumental Rationality," *Southern California Law Review*, V. 46

(1973), pp. 617–660; and A. MacIntyre, *After Virtue: A Study in Moral Theory* (Notre Dame, Ind.: Notre Dame University Press, 1981).

Chapter Five

1. J. Bentham, *An Introduction to the Principles of Morals and Legislation*, J. H. Burns and H. L. A. Hart, eds. (London: University of London Press, 1970), p. 11 (first published in 1789).

2. J. March, "The Technology of Foolishness," in J. March and J. Olsen (eds.), *Ambiguity and Choice in Organizations* (Bergen: Universitetsforlaget, 1976), p. 69. A similar definition is provided by G. Allison in *The Essence of Decision: Explaining the Cuban Missile Crisis* (Boston: Little, Brown, 1971), pp. 29–30.

3. See A. MacIntyre, "Utilitarianism and Cost-Benefit Analysis: An Essay on the Relevance of Moral Philosophy to Bureaucratic Theory," in K. Sayer (ed.), *Values in the Electric Power Industry* (Notre Dame, Ind.: Notre Dame University Press, 1977), pp. 217–237; I. R. Hoos, *Systems Analysis in Public Policy*, rev. ed. (Los Angeles: University of California Press, 1983) (first edition published in 1972); and P. Taylor, *Principles of Ethics: An Introduction* (Encino, Calif.: Dickenson, 1975).

4. H. Simon, "A Behavioral Model of Rational Choice," *Quarterly Journal of Economics*, V. 69 (1955), pp. 99–118; H. Simon, "Rational Choice and the Structure of the Environment," *Psychological Review*, V. 63 (1956), pp. 129–138.

5. C. E. Lindblom, "The Science of 'Muddling Through,'" *Public Administration Review*, V. 19 (1959), pp. 120–128.

6. R. M. Cyert and J. G. March, *A Behavioral Theory of the Firm* (Englewood Cliffs, N.J.: Prentice-Hall, 1963).

7. P. O. Soelberg, "Unprogrammed Decision Making," *Industrial Management Review*, V. 8 (1967), pp. 19–29.

8. See M. D. Cohen, J. G. March, and J. P. Olsen, "A Garbage Can Model of Organizational Choice," *Administrative*

Science Quarterly, V. 17 (1972), pp. 1–25; H. Mintzberg, D. Raisinghani, and A. Theoret, "The Structure of 'Unstructured' Decision Processes, *Administrative Science Quarterly*, V. 21 (1976), pp. 246–275; and L. Fahey, "Strategic Management Decision Processes," *Strategic Management Journal*, V. 2 (1981), pp. 43–60.

9. A. Downs, "Comments on Urban Renewal Programs," in R. Dorfman (ed.), *Measuring Benefits of Government Investments* (Washington, D.C.: The Brookings Institution, 1965), p. 351.

10. See also B. Hedberg, P. Nystrom, and W. Starbuck, "Camping on Seesaws: Prescriptions for a Self-Designing Organization," *Administrative Science Quarterly*, V. 21 (1976), p. 62.

11. R. A. Heiner, "The Origin of Predictable Behavior," *American Economic Review*, V. 73 (1983), pp. 560–595.

12. J. Elster, *Ulysses and the Sirens: Studies in Rationality and Irrationality*, rev. ed. (London: Cambridge University Press, 1984).

13. A. MacIntyre, *After Virtue*, 2nd ed. (Notre Dame, Ind.: University of Notre Dame Press, 1984), p. 198.

14. E. L. Pincoffs, *Quandaries and Virtues: Against Reductivism in Ethics* (Lawrence, Kan.: University Press of Kansas, 1986).

15. H. Mintzberg et al., p. 266.

16. H. Mintzberg et al., p. 266.

17. H. Mintzberg et al., p. 266.

18. L. B. Johnson, "The Quality of American Government," *Weekly Compilation of Presidential Documents*, V. 3 (March 20, 1967), p. 486.

19. H. Mintzberg et al., p. 258.

20. P. O. Soelberg, p. 26.

21. L. Fahey, pp. 43–60.

22. J. March, p. 72.

23. I. Mitroff and J. Emshoff, "On Strategic Assumption-Making: A Dialectical Approach to Policy and Planning," *Academy of Management Review*, V. 4 (1979), p. 10.

24. C. E. Lindblom, p. 126.

25. C. R. Schwenk, "Cognitive Simplification Processes in Strategic Decision Making," *Strategic Management Journal*, V. 5 (1984), pp. 111–128.

26. K. Popper, *Conjectures and Refutations: The Growth of Scientific Knowledge* (New York: Basic Books, 1962).

27. A. Elbing, *Behavioral Decisions in Organizations*, 2nd ed. (Glenview, Ill.: Scott, Foresman, 1978), p. 458.

28. T. B. Bottomore, *Karl Marx: Selected Writings in Sociology and Social Psychology* (New York: McGraw-Hill, 1956), p. 156.

29. L. Tribe, "Ways Not to Think About Plastic Trees: New Foundations for Environmental Law," *The Yale Law Journal*, V. 83 (1974), p. 1332.

30. K. Vonnegut, *Player Piano* (New York: Dell, 1952).

31. M. Pastin, *The Hard Problems of Management: Gaining the Ethics Edge* (San Francisco: Jossey-Bass, 1986), pp. 72–73.

Chapter Six

In an earlier form, this chapter was published as "Practical Formalism: A New Methodological Proposal in Business Ethics," *Journal of Business Ethics*, V. 7 (1988), pp. 163–170.

1. I. Kant, *On the Old Saw: That May Be Right in Theory But It Won't Work in Practice*, E. B. Ashton, trans. (Philadelphia: University of Pennsylvania Press, 1974) (originally published in 1793).

2. See V. Barry, *Moral Issues in Business* (Belmont, Calif.: Wadsworth, 1986), p. 58; and T. Beauchamp and N. Bowie (eds.), *Ethical Theory and Business* (Englewood Cliffs, N.J.: Prentice-Hall, 1983), p. 33.

3. G. F. Cavanagh, D. J. Moberg, and M. Velasquez, "The Ethics of Organizational Politics," *Academy of Management Review*, V. 6 (1981), pp. 363–374; K. Davis and W. C. Frederick, *Business and Society: Management, Public Policy, Ethics* (New York: McGraw-Hill, 1984); G. F. Cavanagh,

American Business Values (Englewood Cliffs, N.J.: Prentice-Hall, 1984); and M. Velasquez, *Business Ethics: Concepts and Cases* (Englewood Cliffs, N.J.: Prentice-Hall, 1982).

4. G. F. Cavanagh, pp. 18–22.

5. J. Rohr, *Ethics for Bureaucrats: An Essay on Law and Values* (New York: Marcel Dekker, 1978).

6. R. DeGeorge, "The Environment, Rights, and Future Generations," in K. E. Goodpaster and K. M. Sayer (eds.), *Ethics and Problems of the Twenty-First Century*, 2nd ed. (Notre Dame, Ind.: University of Notre Dame Press, 1979).

7. J. J. Thomson, "Preferential Hiring," *Philosophy and Public Affairs*, V. 2 (1973), p. 380.

8. A. Z. Carr, "Is Business Bluffing Ethical?" *Harvard Business Review*, V. 46 (1968), p. 146.

9. P. Drucker, "Ethical Chic," *Forbes* (September 14, 1981), p. 161.

10. K. Weick, *The Social Psychology of Organizing*, 2nd ed. (Menlo Park, Calif.: Addison-Wesley, 1979), pp. 47–48.

11. M. Velasquez, p. 67.

12. L. Tribe, "Ways Not to Think About Plastic Trees: New Foundations for Environmental Law," *The Yale Law Journal*, V. 83 (1974), p. 1332.

13. C. Stone, "Should Trees Have Standing: Toward Legal Rights for Natural Objects," *Southern California Law Review*, V. 45 (1972), pp. 453–460, 463–474, 480–481, 486–487.

14. See F. A. Von Hayek, "The 'Non-Sequitur' of the 'Dependence Effect,'" in T. Beauchamp and N. Bowie (eds.), *Ethical Theory and Business*, 3rd ed. (Englewood Cliffs, N.J.: Prentice Hall, 1988), pp. 410–413; and J. K. Galbraith, *The Affluent Society* (New York: Houghton-Mifflin, 1958), pp. 124–130.

15. J. Rawls, *A Theory of Justice* (Cambridge, Mass.: The Belknap Press of Harvard University Press, 1971), pp. 17–22.

16. R. Nozick, *Anarchy, State, and Utopia* (New York: Basic Books, 1974), pp. 10–11.

17. S. Benn, "Freedom and Persuasion," in T. Beauchamp and N. Bowie (eds.), *Ethical Theory and Business* (Englewood Cliffs, N.J.: Prentice-Hall, 1983), p. 374.

18. M. Friedman, "The Social Responsibility of Business Is to Increase Its Profits," *New York Times Magazine* (Sept. 13, 1970), pp. 32–33, 122–126.

19. See, for example, K. Goodpaster and J. Matthews, "Can a Corporation Have a Conscience?" *Harvard Business Review*, V. 60 (1982), pp. 132–141; and K. Davis, "An Expanded View of the Social Responsibility of Business," *Business Horizons*, V. 18 (1975), pp. 19–24.

20. I. Kant, *Foundations of the Metaphysic of Morals*, L. W. Beck, trans. (New York: Bobbs-Merrill, 1959), p. 39 (originally published in 1785).

21. I. Kant, 1959, pp. 39–41.

22. See O. Nell, *Acting on Principles: An Essay in Kantian Ethics* (New York: Columbia University Press, 1975); R. M. Hare, *Freedom and Reason* (London: Oxford University Press, 1963); and M. G. Singer, *Generalization in Ethics* (New York: Alfred A. Knopf, 1961).

23. N. Daniels, "Wide Reflective Equilibrium and Theory Acceptance in Ethics," *Journal of Philosophy*, V. 2 (1979), pp. 256–282.

24. D. Lyons, *Forms and Limits of Utilitarianism* (Oxford: Clarendon Press, 1965), p. 37.

25. A. N. Whitehead, *Process and Reality* (New York: Macmillan, 1929), p. 7.

26. See, for example, F. N. Brady, "A Janus-Headed Model of Ethical Theory: Looking Two Ways at Business-Society Issues," *Academy of Management Review*, V. 10 (1985), pp. 568–576.

27. R. T. DeGeorge, *Business Ethics* (New York: Macmillan, 1986), pp. 67–68.

28. A. J. Bahm, "Teaching Ethics Without Ethics to Teach," *Journal of Business Ethics*, V. 1 (1982), pp. 43–47.

29. P. Drucker, p. 173.

Chapter Seven

In an earlier form, this chapter was published as "Rules for Making Exceptions to Rules," *The Academy of Management Review*, V. 12 (1987), pp. 436–444.

1. A. N. Whitehead, *Process and Reality* (New York: The Free Press, 1929), p. 10.

2. T. Peters and R. Waterman, *In Search of Excellence* (New York: Harper & Row, 1982), pp. 318–326.

3. V. Thompson, *Modern Organizations* (New York: Alfred A. Knopf, 1961), p. 152.

4. R. K. Merton, *Social Theory and Social Structure* (Glencoe, Ill.: The Free Press, 1957), p. 197.

5. C. B. Perrow, *Organizational Analysis: A Sociological View* (Belmont, Calif.: Wadsworth, 1970).

6. H. A. Simon, *Model of Man* (New York: Wiley, 1957).

7. R. Heiner, "The Origins of Predictable Behavior," *American Economic Review*, V. 73 (1983), pp. 560–595.

8. See P. Taylor, *Principles of Ethics: An Introduction* (Encino, Calif.: Dickenson, 1975); I. Kant, *Foundation of a Metaphysic of Morals*, L. W. Beck, trans. (New York: Bobbs-Merrill, 1959) (originally published in 1785); and J. Bentham, *An Introduction to the Principles of Morals and Legislation* (Oxford: Clarendon Press, 1897) (originally published in 1789).

9. E. F. Schumacher, *A Guide for the Perplexed* (New York: Harper & Row, 1977), p. 123.

10. A. M. Okun, *Equality and Efficiency: The Big Tradeoff* (Washington, D.C.: The Brookings Institution, 1975).

11. J. Rawls, *A Theory of Justice* (Cambridge, Mass.: Harvard University Press, 1971), p. 60.

12. A. MacIntyre, "Utilitarianism and Cost-Benefit Analysis: An Essay on the Relevance of Moral Philosophy to Bureaucratic Theory," in K. Sayer (ed.), *Values in the Electric Power Industry* (Notre Dame, Ind.: University of Notre Dame Press, 1977); see also, P. Taylor, p. 12–22.

13. See P. Taylor, p. 19; R. Nozick, *Anarchy, State, and Utopia* (New York: Basic Books, 1974), pp. 153–155; and J. Rawls, p. 22–27.

14. V. Thompson, p. 153.

15. C. B. Perrow, *Complex Organizations*, 3rd ed. (New York: Random House, 1986), pp. 7–9.

16. J. Elster, *Ulysses and the Sirens: Studies in Rationality and Irrationality*, rev. ed. (Cambridge: Cambridge University Press, 1984), p. 109.

17. T. Peters and R. Waterman, pp. 318–326.

18. R. T. Pascale and A. G. Athos, *The Art of Japanese Management: Applications for American Executives* (New York: Warner Books, 1981), p. 151.

19. D. Lyons, *Forms and Limits of Utilitarianism* (Oxford: Clarendon Press, 1965).

20. M. Dalton, *Men Who Manage* (New York: Wiley, 1959).

21. L. H. Tribe, "Technology Assessment and the Fourth Discontinuity: The Limits of Instrumental Rationality," *Southern California Law Review*, V. 46 (1973), pp. 631–632.

Chapter Eight

In an earlier form, this chapter was published as "The Aesthetic Components of Management Ethics," *The Academy of Management Review*, V. 11 (1986), pp. 337–344.

1. G. Ryle, *The Concept of Mind* (London: Hutchinson's University Library, 1949).

2. G. Ryle, pp. 48–49.

3. G. Ryle, p. 54.

4. M. Polanyi, *The Tacit Dimension* (Garden City, N.Y.: Doubleday, 1966), p. 4.

5. M. Polanyi, *Personal Knowledge* (Chicago: University of Chicago Press, 1958).

6. H. Reichenback, *The Rise of Scientific Philosophy* (Berkeley: University of California Press, 1951), p. 231.

7. J. P. Sartre, *Being and Nothingness* (New York: Citadel Press, 1956).

8. M. Polanyi, 1966, p. 7.

9. S. P. Springer and G. Deutsch, *Left Brain, Right Brain* (New York: Freeman, 1981), p. 185.

10. W. Barrett, *The Illusion of Technique* (New York: Doubleday, 1967).

11. C. Hartshorne, "Beyond Enlightened Self-Interest," *Ethics*, V. 84 (1974), p. 214.

12. A. N. Whitehead, *Modes of Thought* (New York: Macmillan, 1938), p. 14.

13. A. N. Whitehead, *The Aims of Education and Other Essays* (New York: Macmillan, 1929), p. 14.

14. R. Pascale and A. Athos, *The Art of Japanese Management: Applications for American Executives* (New York: Warner Books, 1981), pp. 131–182.

15. R. Pascale and A. Athos, p. 151.

16. M. P. Maccoby, *The Gamesman* (New York: Simon & Schuster, 1976), p. 125.

17. T. Peters and R. Waterman, *In Search of Excellence* (New York: Harper & Row, 1982), pp. 318–326.

18. R. M. Hare, *Moral Thinking* (New York: Oxford University Press, 1981), p. 25.

19. C. Hodgkinson, *Toward a Philosophy of Administration* (New York: St. Martin's Press, 1978), pp. 221–222.

20. W. Barrett, *The Illusion of Technique* (New York: Doubleday, 1967), p. 26.

Chapter Nine

1. A. Carr, "Is Business Bluffing Ethical?" *Harvard Business Review*, V. 46 (1968), pp. 145–153.

2. A. Carr, p. 153.

3. F. Knight, "The Ethics of Competition," *The Quarterly Journal of Economics*, V. 37 (1935), pp. 579–624.

4. R. Jackall, *Moral Mazes: The World of Corporate Managers* (New York: Oxford University Press, 1988), p. 49.

5. R. Jackall, pp. 50–56.

6. R. Jackall, p. 204.

7. R. Jackall, pp. 91–92.

8. R. Jackall, p. 68.

9. M. Kennedy, *Office Warfare: Strategies for Getting Ahead in the Aggressive 80's* (New York: Macmillan, 1985), pp. 133–137.

10. M. Kennedy, p. 134.

11. M. Kennedy, p. 153.

12. H. Mackay, *Swim with the Sharks Without Being Eaten Alive* (New York: William Morrow, 1988), p. 66.

13. H. Mackay, pp. 106–107.

14. R. Jackall, p. 121.

15. H. Spencer, *Social Statics* (London: Appleton, 1850).

16. R. Pascale and A. Athos, *The Art of Japanese Management: Applications for American Executives* (New York: Warner Books, 1981), pp. 183–238.

17. J. Elster, *Ulysses and the Sirens: Studies in Rationality and Irrationality* rev. ed. (Cambridge: Cambridge University Press, 1984), p. 20.

Appendix

Survey of Ethical Theoretic Aptitudes

Instructions: Each of the following statements can be completed in two ways. Think about each alternative, and circle the one that you think best represents your feelings.

1. Persons' actions should be described in terms of being
   a. good or bad.
   b. right or wrong.
2. When making an ethical decision, one should pay attention to
   a. one's conscience.
   b. others' needs, wants, and desires.
3. Solutions to ethical problems are usually
   a. some shade of gray.
   b. black and white.
4. It is of more value to societies to
   a. follow stable traditions and maintain a distinctive identity.
   b. be responsive and adapt to new conditions as the world changes.

5. When thinking through ethical problems, I prefer to
   a. develop practical, workable alternatives.
   b. make reasonable distinctions and clarifications.

6. When people disagree over ethical matters, I strive for
   a. some point(s) of agreement.
   b. workable compromises.

7. Uttering a falsehood is wrong because
   a. depending on the results, it can lead to further problems.
   b. it wouldn't be right for anyone to lie.

8. Thinking of occupations, I would rather be a
   a. wise judge, applying the law with fairness and impartiality.
   b. benevolent legislator, seeking an improved life for all.

9. I would rather be known as a person who
   a. has accomplished a lot and achieved much.
   b. has integrity and is a person of principle.

10. The aim of science should be
    a. to discover truth.
    b. to solve existing problems.

11. Whether a person is a liar is
    a. a matter of degree.
    b. a question of kind.

12. A nation should pay more attention to its
    a. heritage, its roots.
    b. its future, its potential.

13. It is more important to be
    a. happy.
    b. worthy.

14. Unethical behavior is best described as
    a. violation of a principle of law.
    b. causing some degree of harm.

15. The purpose of government should be
    a. to promote the best possible life for its citizens.
    b. to secure justice and fair treatment.

How to Score this Test

<u>SCORE = Odd As + Even Bs − 8</u>

+7 ≥ Score ≥ +5: "flaming utilitarian"
+4 ≥ Score ≥ +2: "moderate utilitarian"
+1 ≥ Score ≥ −1: "mugwump"
−2 ≥ Score ≥ −4: "moderate formalist"
−5 ≥ Score ≥ −8: "ice-cold formalist"

This diagnostic test has been used for many years in many settings, both in the academic world and in the private and public sectors. It is designed to ascertain an individual's inclination to approach ethical issues from a formalist or a utilitarian perspective. There are no wrong answers and no unethical scores. About 90 percent of respondants score in the +5 to −5 range.

When you have taken the test, compare your score with those of others around you. Do the similarities or differences in scores account for any intuited features in yourself or others?

Index